LALITAMBA

Issue 3

Cover art by Shinjo Ito

ISBN 978-0-9778633-2-7
ISSN 1930-0662

The name for the journal was inspired by a devotional song, "Lalitamba, Lalitamba," sung on a pilgrimage through India. In the winter of 2004, we traveled through the country in an effort to alleviate the suffering that comes with poverty, illness, and loss of hope. During our travels was born the idea for a literary magazine that would uplift the spirit. The name Lalitamba means Divine Mother. In India, the Divine Mother is thought of as *jagado dharini,* or She who supports the universe.

Submission Guidelines: Please submit up to five poems or pieces of art, or one work of prose, per envelope. Work should be previously unpublished. Please include SASE and contact information, including email address. We accept submissions by mail at *Lalitamba*, P.O. Box 131, Planetarium Station, New York, New York, 10024.

Subscriptions are $10 for one biannual issue, plus $4.50 postage and handling. Please make checks payable to Lalitamba Mandiram.

Please address all editorial correspondence to *Lalitamba*, P.O. Box 131, Planetarium Station, New York, New York 10024. Ph. 212.873.0140. E. info@lalitamba.org.

TABLE OF CONTENTS

Interviews

Poetry

LETTERS AND PRAYERS

Dear God,

Please help those who are suffering in the street, with no place to go or food to eat. God bless those who are sick. Bless those who have lost their loved ones on 9/11. Give them strength to hold on, to know that you are with them when they're down and out. Please help people from New Orleans find a place to go. Help the troops to come back home. Please stop the war in Iraq. And give peace and love and joy to those who have no one. Help the navy and the army, and give toys to their families. I pray for the people in prison, for those who did not commit a crime. God, please bless and keep our families safe. I pray for my children. They are in foster care. I love them with all my heart.

Marilyn Pierce
New York, NY

Beloved,

I need you to know how angry I am that my family has broken apart. That family was mine. You gave it to me. And then you took it, and you broke it, and you did not fix it.

My family is not a teacup, of fragile beauty yet easily forgotten. My family is not some souvenir trinket of which I would have tired. And I had only one.

With that family, my feeling of belonging anywhere in this world has been destroyed. So has my belief in fairy-tale endings. My trust has been battered as if it were a prayer flag torn against the rocks.

You are the one who calms all storms. You are the one who saves. Where are your miracles? I am waiting for you to answer.

Yours,
Mary H.
Los Angeles, CA

MY OATH TO YOU...

When you are sad…I will dry your tears.
When you are scared…I will comfort your fears.
When you are worried…I will give you hope.
When you are confused…I will help you cope.
And when you are lost…And can't see the light,
I shall be your beacon…Shining ever so bright.
This is my oath…I pledge till the end.

Signed: GOD

The journal is for the One I love.

Carl Alessi

Love and Flowers

SAN FRANCISCO 1967—On January 14, over twenty thousand seekers and flower children gather in Golden Gate Park for the "First Human Be-In." They come with happy painted faces and garbed in colorful costumes. Beat poets and spirit leaders of the young generation. Allen Ginsberg and Gary Snyder begin the day by chanting *mantra*. The best of the new psychedelic rock bands play music all day. The Diggers give out hundreds of free sandwiches to the crowd.

Local poet Lenore Kandel reads and then announces, "Here, today, in this place, a new era is dawning. The God of this era is love!" Even the fearsome Hell's Angels seem touched by the spiritual currents. They volunteer to guard the sound system. Everywhere are smiling faces—barefoot girls in monk's cloaks and teenage "braves" stripped to the waist. Motorcyclists, vagabonds, street poets, and infants.

The master of ceremonies announces from the flower-strewn stage, "Brothers, the spirit of the new Messiah may not be coming to us, but from us."

With the golden sun setting, Allen Ginsberg and Gary Snyder chant in the approaching night with *om sri maitreya*. Soon, the magical day is over.

The last voice from the stage is Allen Ginsberg's: "Look down now at your feet and practice a little kitchen yoga after this first American *mehla*. Please pick up all refuse you see about you. Shantih."

Has the new Aquarian Age begun here? Some will say, yes.

Ben Wilensky

Before the Beginning

Creating Everything from Nothing
is a redaction of a translation of a lost original
and sets the stage for complex comedy.

When God Began to Create
implies the Creator was not always creating
and even before this beginning began the Bible claims
the earth existed as a rude amorphous lump
blownthiswaythatwayupandownbyawesomeanarchicwinds.

This   whistlingdump   was a *toyvoo vi voyhoo*   a voice on top of a void
a waste on top of a waste   squatting and sitting   voiding and wasting
in never-ending cycles of excretion.
Was our Great Creator a mighty punster and a prankster
provoking lumps of clay into becoming their own sparks of divinity?

Tradition tells us the *toyvoo* is often troubled and sits by itself
and in its stark isolation descends even further
down into the deepest darkest holes of depression
smearing the walls around it with hopeless despair.

Pivotal questions are then presented to our fathers:
Is this world absurd? And is God a failed creator?
Is it possible God is the one doing all the despairing?
And what about our mothers?

We who are not born yet
must answer the seminal question of our unborn lives:
Is life worth living in this weltering waste
and if the answer is *yes*
then how do we make a difference?

No other living thing exists before that beginning
and yet the written word places human sensibilities
right in the middle of this daunting stink.

Beginnings shroud themselves in boisterous sweat.
Endings come hard and fast with icy remoteness.
Somewhere in the center of these bipolar extremities
the search goes on for viability.

Our human condition is befuddled.
By constant re-invention we prepare the way for spirited self-mockery.

Demons who once chewed on human fat
are now stuffed and mounted high up on a wall and there they hang
terrifying children into obeisance.

When words were first grunted into legends
they were drawn from the moaning groans
of dying spirits
then fused with the souls of aspiring creators
obsessed with breathing new life into contradictions.

Insignificant bugs adhered to an insignificant feather
then feathers adhered to a bird and birds to an eagle
and eagles to a mighty wind rising high up above the void
until all of us were floating in majestic flight,
balancing for a purpose,
croaking poems of possibilities.

In every momentous beginning radical action splits the sky.
Light streams across the battlefield with shattering illumination
and by this electrical shock
some of us separate chaff from wheat and bake a new kind of bread
trembling in the way we change ordinary blood into unparalleled cake.

But who eats what and who does not demands responsibility.

Appalled by insane solutions to acts of dying
we watch bodies crumble and brickface tumble down into mortifying dust.
We sanitize decay with bits of rouge and white paint but nothing works.

We summon memories of those still living in the past
those we loved and lost and how we miss them still
hoping they will open up their arms and welcome us to paradise.

We join a church and pray the light burns brighter
and more inclusive as we pass away
but there's always one comedian in the crowd who claims
toyvoo vi voyhoo is nothing
but a blast from the past
and we poor players fodder for the fuel.

Tongue-tied I am forever searching for my glasses.
How can I see when I keep banging into walls without my glasses?

Fortunately I am married to a steadfast wife
who raises the windows and helps me inhale the morning air.

We slap red mud and throw the clay into pots that smack of consequence
and even if a pot should break
or spirits leak onto the ground
creation makes a difference.

Adrienne Amundsen

Song

In the beginning I sang.
Sitting high in a mountain
monastery,
butter tea,
high sky, ice blue,
cerulean,
I sang.

I sang Tara, all love, her golden heart,
her pulse,
her golden light,
pouring, pulsing,
spilling over the temple walls,
down mountain sides,
down the valleys,
across the world.
I sang
the song without end.

After many years I began to awaken.
I saw a woman open her mouth
to take in her lover's tongue.
I felt her body melt in magenta waves,
hearts pound,
rising roar,
skin shudder with a sound
like snakes on sand.
I saw,
I saw her belly swell.
I saw a baby
come crowning out of the dark.
I heard her screaming,

smelled blood, molten, tearing,
wild torment.
I saw joy.

I saw a mother touch her baby's hot pink mouth
and watched their smiles bloom like flowers.
I saw sweet milk
beading on a nipple's tip,
the baby tongue lapping.

I saw a young girl racing through sunflowers
on a bay mare's back,
her legs sweeping in rhythm along the horse's side.
I saw
sunflowers high as trees.
I saw the mare,
muscular,
carry the girl,
red colt at their side.
Cicadas hummed,
and the air smelled of sun and oak
and heat.

I wanted that.

So I poured myself down the mountainside.
Like waves of honey, or
harmonic
lava,
I flowed.

And then—
oh then—
I saw a mother sitting by a small corpse,
ocean's roar pouring forth from her
mouth, open like a black cave,
a sound crashing on my new ears
like thunder, like
an explosion.
I saw a mother touch her baby's rosebud mouth,
bleeding,
and erupt in wailing so loud
I could not hear the song anymore.
I saw, I saw
things I did not grasp.
Why does this boy carry a gun,
this building burn,

these people flee,
empty eyes, black holes,
bottomless,
blinded?
I see herds, hordes,
roaming open roads
past poisoned pools
where fish are dying.
I see smoke,
I see crosses,
I see fields of the dead
and storms of stars raining down from great silver. It looks like a bird,
but it rains pain.
I see,
I see
the carrion birds
over the fields of the fallen.

I cannot hear my song.
It is drowned in the cries and the roar.
I cannot hear my song.
It is gone,
and I join the crowd of refugees walking.
I walk.

I feel my flat belly groan and pull.
Bags on my back,
I hold the hands of my
children.
We walk.

Night falls:
We stop by the roadside.
I pull meager bread and honey from my bag,
place it like nectar in their open mouths.
They gape like hatchlings.
I pull them to me,
hold them tightly to me.
I hold them,
and I begin to hum.
I begin to sing.
I sing.

Once I sang you into being,
and I poured myself out to find you.
I found you, but I found
sorrow too,
and blood and hunger.
Once I sang only light and honey.

I sang heart.
I sang.
In the beginning
I sang.

Bhau Kalchuri

Lover and Beloved

Oh Meher, God-Incarnate
this is dedicated to the Original Song
to be tuned by everyone in the creation
to fulfill the purpose of life.

It was summer in Poona, April 1968, and by early morning it was already hot. I sat directly under the fan in my room upstairs at Guruprasad with a copy of *The Wayfarers*, which I was translating from English into Hindi. I did not enjoy this translation work, but since Baba had asked me at Meherazad to do it, I had begun the translation as soon as the Mandali and Baba had settled in at Guruprasad.

On this day in April, which was to give birth to *Meher Sarod*, I continued working through lunch as usual on the translation, not joining the other men downstairs. Looking out the window, I thought of all the lovers who would miss having Baba's *darshan* this year.

Baba had declared that He would not give public *darshan* at Guruprasad, and He even had signs posted on the gates of Guruprasad stating, "Avatar Meher Baba Has Stopped Seeing or Giving Darshan to Anyone." He had also instructed the Mandali that none of us were to leave the grounds.

Instead of the usual morning meetings and *darshan* at Guruprasad, Baba was working in His room in strict seclusion, with orders for absolute silence in the building and on the grounds. After doing the inner work alone for several hours, Baba would walk into the main hall and call for the Mandali. Baba would appear exhausted and weak as a result of His seclusion work. The Mandali would then join Baba in prayers—"The Prayer of Repentance" and "The Master's Prayer." This was the daily routine, and no one from outside was allowed in. I was exempt from these morning sessions because of the writing Baba had instructed me to complete. But at 2:45 every afternoon, I would close the notebooks. I would go to be with Baba and attend to Him in His room from three o'clock until eight in the evening.

Later, waiting on the verandah to be called into Baba's room, I squinted at the traffic on the road. Three o'clock was the hottest time of the day, and the afternoon sun blazed on the open patches of lawn and street.

Inside, Baba's room was suffocating. Stepping into it was like walking into an oven. Every ventilator, window, and door was tightly shut by Baba's order. Baba sat on His bed, relaxed, in His long undershorts without a shirt. His forehead and arms were covered with perspiration. I took a handkerchief and wiped Baba's brow, as He inquired about the day's writing work and remarked about what had happened in the morning with the other Mandali.

Baba was in a good mood, sitting on His bed. At about 6:30, as the evening twilight came, He gestured, "Today I will teach you how to write *ghazals*."

I was sweating profusely in the ninety-degree heat and did not say anything in reply. I had protested against writing *ghazals* previously, but Baba would not let the subject drop. "What's the use of arguing?" I thought. "Let Baba do what He likes."

At Meherazad, over a year earlier, Baba had said, "I want you to write *ghazals* in Hindi." Surprised, I had replied, "Baba, it isn't possible. *Ghazals* can only be written in Persian or Urdu, not in Hindi or in any other language." Baba did not like my reply. "What do you take Me for?" He gestured. "I am Ustad—the Master. I taught [Dr.] Ghani to write *ghazals* and I will teach you; but you must try."

I had tried, and the result was a hundred and eighty-five songs titled *Meher Geetika*. Baba had liked the poems very much, but He had remarked, "They are not *ghazals* but only *ghazal*-like."

Now Baba said to me, "You have written with all your heart in *Meher Geetika* and the songs are good, but I want you to write real *ghazals*, and today I will teach you. I will give you one line, and I want you to repeat this line to the rhythm I will beat out."

Baba then dictated this line: "Now my heart is terrified even to hear the name of Love."

I began repeating it slowly to Baba, as Baba played a rhythm with His fist on His thighs like a *tabla*. "Now my heart is terrified even to hear the name of Love… Now my heart is terrified…"

Standing before Baba in the intense heat, I repeated this line over and over again. Half an hour passed. I was perspiring, and Baba was also perspiring as He repeated and repeated the rhythm. But I could not grasp the rhythm which Baba was trying to make me understand. After awhile I pleaded, "Baba, I do not follow; please do not take so much trouble for me."

Baba gave me a sharp glance while never stopping His constant rhythmic pounding, and He gestured, "Continue, continue." So I continued to repeat the line to Baba for another half-hour. "Now my heart is terrified even to hear the name of Love." Despite the repetition, I still had no notion of the meter Baba was strenuously trying to make me grasp. Again I pleaded, "Baba, it is too hot in here; please stop this."

But Baba would not hear of it, and again gestured, "Continue, continue." For another fifteen minutes the sound of Baba's thigh-slapping rhythm to my monotonous repetition of the same line went on. I became more and more exasperated during this final fifteen minutes. I found it difficult to concentrate because of the oppressive heat. As I said, Baba was also soaked with perspiration from the continuous exertion. It had been going on for an hour and fifteen minutes. Finally I could not contain myself any longer, and I blurted out, "Baba, please stop now; I cannot follow a thing."

This time Baba looked at me with disgust and gestured, "You're useless! Go and sit down." With this, Baba lay back on His bed, but continued hitting His thighs with His fists in the same fashion.

I sat in a chair and looked at Baba who was lying on His back beating out the *ghazal* rhythm on His thighs. I thought, "What a nut I am. I simply cannot follow what Baba wants me to understand. Baba took so much trouble for me, but still I cannot understand. How can I compose *ghazals* in Hindi? It's impossible."

Then something wonderful happened. As I sat in the chair with these thoughts, all of a sudden—like a gust of wind—understanding came to me. Instantly I knew what Baba wanted. I knew how to write *ghazals*, the meters and the composition!

In turn, without saying a word, Baba immediately sat up and, quickly snapping His fingers, He gestured, "Now compose!" Then and there, in five minutes, I wrote the first *ghazal* of *Meher Sarod* and read it out to Baba. Baba embraced me and said, "Yes, this is what I want." Tapping my head with His fingers, Baba continued, "This is what I was trying to make your hard 'nut' understand. From now on I will give you a line or so every day, and you should continue composing in this way."

The italicized couplets in the following ghazals were given to Bhauji by Meher Baba.

Bhau Kalchuri

The Parrot Is Freed

Oh Meher, what has happened to my heart's cup?
I am weeping to find it empty.

One is fortunate who draws You close.
One finds You by turning into dust.

Wine is flowing from Your glance,
But only a head that is bowed can drink it.

How can I forget You oh Beloved?
Your arrow is still in my heart.

When Your pleasure is sought, everything is found.
The cage door is opened and the parrot is freed.

Bhau's life faces a barren autumn;
He is so helpless, he can only laugh.

Bhau Kalchuri

I Gained After Becoming Dust

My life has become alive from Your sweet remembrance,
Oh Beloved Meher, wherever You are there is light.

Oh the wine You gave me! One sip of Your wine inflamed my heart.
My nest is burning and the parrot now weeps.

Oh what power is in Your glance!
It made me helpless—absorbed and lost in You.

You keep Yourself hidden behind the curtain,
Yet You always claim You never veil Yourself.

What have I gained after becoming dust?
I lost all wants—His wish became my will.

Oh Bhau, the Beloved does not hear even the song of dust.
For lifetimes He has not responded to my dust
    singing at His doorstep.

Bhau Kalchuri

Repeatedly Birth After Death

Oh Meher, let me drink the wine flowing from Your eyes.
I have come a great distance, repeatedly changing clothes.

Oh Beloved, be with me at every step—
I have failed thousands of times trying to proceed on my own.

Accept my life as a flower in Your garden.
Though I am still a bud, allow me to bloom.

I have spent my life searching for Your abode
Only to realize that I will never find it
    without You as my companion.

You are my only source of help—I belong to You completely.
If you do not believe me, test me by changing Your moods.

I know that You only shower mercy on fire—not tears.
But, oh Beloved, the tears You see are from the fire in my heart.

Oh Bhau, why is the moment of union always being postponed?
My life is only of two days—
    how can I enjoy His union after it ends?

Bhau Kalchuri

Weeping in Your Remembrance

Oh Beloved Meher, I am weeping in Your remembrance
And my heart is deeply wounded by the fire of my tears.

The Path will be lit if I hold Your hand in mine—
But, oh Beloved, how can something so elusive be grasped?

Your remembrance has ignited a fire in my heart;
Remain awake there and let me sleep forever.

Whatever I once remembered—I am now forgetting.
But tell me, is this the way of finding or losing You?

If I have the pain of Your longing
  the three worlds will come under my command.
You will remain in the company of my heart,
  its wounds You cannot avoid.

Oh Bhau, I finally decided to wash my clothes
  on the stone of His love.
Seeing me labor, my Beloved gave me the nectar of love as soap.

Bhau Kalchuri

The Pain Brings Me to You

Oh Meher, Your remembrance pervades in my tears
And this downpour lights a fire in my heart.

My mind retreats from the pain, but Your love draws me on to You.
At every step You console me, "The destination is right here."

I am walking day and night without rest,
And You tell me the destination is where I am.

Mid-ocean's turbulence has become the shore
Since Your hand came into mine; but now the destination follows me.

Oh Beloved, I love Your pain more than I love You—
You are indifferent, while the pain brings me to You.

Oh Bhau, I am so restless I do not know what to do,
But now I find my Beloved is with me all the time.

Bhau Kalchuri's writings have been reprinted with his permission from the book
Meher Sarod (Manifestation, 1984).

Gabriella Tal

with Bhau

for Bhau Kalchuri

We quiver as one heart
ready for the
        arrow you sling
        opening us to that
        essential longing
        to the bliss that drips
        off the edges of words
        and that we see
        in the innocent shape of
            your toes.
Love is palpable
in a room full of lovers
        listening with one ear,
        the beats of
        our hearts drumming
        together as
        one song

like the humming of a great railway car
taking us to station after station,
heading far down the track
into the dark
and welcoming night.

Gabriella Tal

Contentment

for Meher Baba

Tonight I read the book of night
    —as I have often done—
      but I read it differently now.
I feel it
—not with this body—
 but with a body beyond.

How can one describe contentment?
   A raindrop on a leaf,
      thunder speaking from
         the horizon,
      deer hooves on the forest floor
      caressing earth with a thumping sound.
This too—
but these barely touch it.

Contentment is in the heart—
The heart which has ached to be open
now aches in the opening,
an ache that widens the breath
and smiles the eyes.
The depth of my strength grows,
yet I am soft.
Could I have asked for this?

Florence Homolka

Reflections

Purnamadah Purnamidam
Purnat Purnamudachyate
Purnasya Purnamadaya
Purnam Eva Vasisyate
—*Isha Upanishad*

i.
This is perfect. That is perfect.
The perfect brings forth the perfect.
As the perfect recedes,
The perfect remains.

ii.
She is God.
God is She.
God's hand offers
Only God.
When God disappears
Behind the veil of illusion,

She appears to be
Everywhere.

iii.
The seed is One.
The tree is One.
From the One
Comes the One.
When the seed falls away,
The tree stands.
When the tree falls
The seed sprouts.

iv.
The beggar is God.
The bomber is God.
The way to know God
Is to embrace God.
When we turn from God,
God remains
God.

Bobby Minkoff

My Brother the Beggar

Walking to the bookstore on upper Broadway,
I am accompanied by my nineteen-year-old daughter.

We pass a beggar in a wheelchair.
I turn back
and put a few bucks in his cup.
"God bless you," he says.
My daughter tells me
how generous she thinks I was.
I try to explain:

What's the difference
between him and me?
Am I really so worthy, so noble
that I deserve to have
and he so despicable and lowly
that somehow he does not?

Maybe I had better parents
who worked overtime
to pay for my education.

Perhaps, while I got deferred,
he got his legs blown off
in Vietnam.
And when we tripped over life,
I had people to pick me up.
He was left to fall.

The directions of our lives
are unknown and unknowable.
It's a mystery and a blessing
that I am able to give
to my holy brother, the beggar.

My teacher, Reb Shlomo, used to scold us:
"People think nothing of going out to dinner,
spending fifty, a hundred, or more.
But when they pass by a poor person,
they reach no deeper than loose change.
It's a *shanda*,
A terrible crying shame."

Elisavietta Ritchie

Just Before Sunset

To catch the hour of gold in the cove
discard your coins of silver and tin,
platinum buckets, pails with holes,
the circular lens with the metal rim,
all bracelets, even the rings.

Walk out where beach and jetty end,
where waves break in the last rays of sun.
Jump over rocks and crabs.
Step straight into wet and cold
mud-sand beneath the skin of sea.
Follow the black-and-white ducks.
They submerge and surface, dive again,
reappear, shake drops from their wings.
When at last you catch up, unsure where
you are, learn to swim before dark.

Susanne Petermann

Birds

Morning has broken, like the first morning.
Blackbird has spoken, like the first bird.
—Eleanor Farjeon

The first morning of summer,
I drive to work,
and who knows what confluence
of time and space
brings into my view a bird, flying but not traveling,
    beak starward
      cheek against the blue pillow of sky
      wings quick with ecstasy—
more, more! says its whole striving body.

In Seattle for the first time,
I stand on a sidewalk.
A crane with a raptor's beak
attached to the end of its mechanical neck
devours a parking garage.

It reaches carefully and bites,
comes within inches of my hotel next door,
crunches concrete and steel crumbs
onto the lap of the earth.
That neck and that jaw
    tasting dust
    smiling at the thrill of hard
    work done well.

Others stop on the sidewalk, as though we were in a zoo.
Behind me stands a window display
of glass art,
    turquoise glass hat with orange glass flower
    hummingbird caught in a perfect prison
    at the moment of perfect union with fire.

Inside the glass:
A still sky, songs.

Here I am, and here is glass, unafraid.
The metal vulture toils across the street.
Here, I am unafraid to witness a bird
who closed its eyes while making love to the sky.

Susanne Petermann

(Untitled Haiku)

Why am I waiting
for the hurrying to cease
these long, tender days?

Ben Koch

Thanking the Precious One for His Swift Destruction of Illusions

for Khenpo Tsultrim Gyamtso Rinpoche

Rinpoche, like a howling thunder train
your roar of compassion broke my house to bits,
entire rooms splintered from their dream of space,
trustworthy appliances sprawled like toppled monuments,
no walls—and how brisk! What naked breezes stream my face!

Rinpoche, flush with dreams I hit the road,
looping striped highways in circular commutes,
exit after exit arising and melting...
Phit! Phit! Phit! Phit! Four honed arrows—your skillful means—
pierce all inflations; how bizarre, to use my legs for once!

Rinpoche, as a last straw my body seemed firm,
the hum of organs in their heart-thumped orchestra,
the joy of breasts in a hundred earthy tones, ho!
Your blades of *prajna* hacked me like a wild butcher,
How light my trot without that lumpish bag of bones!

Rinpoche, your sun of wisdom begins the melt.
Already parts of me flow like a buoyant stream,
happily freed from their glaciers of clinging,
yet how long the journey to the sea, how many
swift rumbling turns and dark-mouthed forests to beat!

Rinpoche, if, on my journey, I should freeze or meet
a deadening jam, may your sun of wisdom evaporate
my mind-stream to the sky of truth, where,
like a cloud, it washes lost mother beings
in a soft rain of your blessings.

Ayaz Daryl Nielsen

Beloved

for Amma

she asks with her eyes
if you love
in silence

this fool
says "yes"

she asks with her tears
can you love
in silence

I, so foolish
so grateful

silent
  within
    this embrace

Janine Canan

Goddess

for Amma

You laid
The golden egg,
You rolled
The silver disc,
You flew the
Emerald world.
You made all this
And made us too.
Goddess, come back
And tell us why.

Kirk Lumpkin

Prayer Flag

There
    is a small
    high-mountained
    almost treeless
    land
    where
        they used to
        raise their prayers
        on little flags
        that fluttered
        like rectangular
        tree leaves.
That land
    is now occupied
    by a huge
    foreign power
    (that
    is a significant
    trading partner

of this nation
of which I
am a citizen
by birth,
this nation
that now occupies
another land
where prayers rise
in turquoise domes
and squawk
from tinny speakers
on lovely spires).

One day
  may all people
    be free,
may no one
  be bombed
    or tortured,

and may all
  occupations
    cease—
    our presence

here
becoming
relationship
with
this land
and all
that are native
to it;
and may we
one day
live
in a borderless
democracy
of living
beings
where
the churches
are forests
and flagpoles
are trees
whose leaves
are praying
tongues

that lick
the wind
with the language
of love
> *above roots*
>> *reaching deep*
> *into our only*
> *homeland,*
> *this Earth.*

Kirk Lumpkin

Spring

Spring
> has come
> rubbing
> its eager
> blossoms
> along
> these fearful
> bones

and muscles
cramped
and aching
for the returning
heat
to shift
the stiffness
toward
the liquid,
toward
the flow,
toward
the splendorous
sinuosity
of river,
of flame
melting
the armor
between
the inner
and the outer
world.

Michele Heather Pollock

This Is How I Pray

There is a trail that winds through
birch trees, over a small hill, and
comes out upon a broad field
planted with wildflowers. The sun
places its trust in their mercy. The wind
makes love openly with any willing
green thing. Is there a prayer
that feels like this? I'll pray it. I watch
this broad expanse of weedy things.
My tongue stirs with words of gratitude.

Michele Heather Pollock

Everyone Knows the Way to Heaven

When you die you might remark,
"So that was where I was supposed to go,"
but in reality, it doesn't matter.
Everyone knows the way to heaven.
Our souls climb out of the world one by one.

A. J. Naslund

Of God's Nature As Light

And how shall I find my way
through a thicket of light, or even
discern the path alongside the
flowing springs of light? In such
wilderness, where will I be, black
speck that I am, turning my dark

face toward the high and light
flying clouds in a field of light
where brilliant and powerful points
of light distinguish the great and
useful constellations? I am looking
for you, God, as a son, naive in
the factory of work, seeks his dad
at the noon break before the bell
has sounded, lost among mighty
powers that remind him of that
one man who holds his destiny for
good or ill, to bring to him a small
wrapped sandwich or a thermos
of mother's coffee. Where's my
dad in this din, fellows, all? Do
you chance to know him? I am lost
in here, though this is the address
he gave me. In the deep darkness
of his light I am going seeking,
with a useless lantern. It is my
intention to hit the trail, too, to go
there, where illumination illuminates
luminaries until there could be no
darkness of any kind left over ever,

unless at the edges of these woods,
in the small radiant foliage where
some leaf or bud of light blanks out
in its new and innocent gleam
what was before meant to be pure,
untroubled, without a spot of darkness
anywhere, but where trivial, spark-like
shadows fall to the ground without
significant weight, darkness of seeds,
in their own unassuming lightness
blowing out to plant another world
where I, I can see, must, myself grow,
nurtured by intricate patterns, organic,
natural, heavy, obdurate, and dark.

Roger Smith

In Light

The gift of feeling
is the gift of light.

So see now how the new light
feels. Brilliance is touch,
and there is no touch by touching
that was never touched back.

In light I am wrapped by
how I feel, and how I feel
the light by touching me is.

Though we are of an elemental
separateness, we are still
this work of one.

A one it feels carried further
than thought thought ever to go,
unless soul is a thinking of
what other this is.

Light as soul simplifying
its everywhere. Light breathing
a world into a heart,

and where I might live
in this heart is when
the light is.

Justin R. McManus

When the Lights Go Out

When the lights go out,
You're scared of the dark.
You can't see a thing.
You hear something move—
A bump in the night.
(You begin to panic.)
You freak out.
You're afraid that something is coming to get you,
And now, you do see something coming.
You try to run, but
You're frozen with fear.
What is it? You don't know.
Then you realize, when you see the light,
That you're standing at the gates of heaven,
And all it was was the Holy Ghost.

Nancy Owen Nelson

The Long Goodbye

This is about darkness and light. The kind of darkness that settles into the human consciousness when there is a loss or traumatic change. It is known as "the dark night of the soul." The phrase originates from the book of the same name by the mystic St. John of the Cross. The following, from a public forum on the topic, describes this condition:

> "The experience of the dark night is a depression that seems to be without cause—when you find everything that used to bring you contentment runs like sand through your fingers, and you are surrounded by an impenetrable mist from which there is no escape— when your mind turns against you and punishes your every positive

move, crippling action, denying all happiness, purging all feeling but despair and exquisite mental agony."[1]

My dark night of the soul was the transition from a life in Michigan to a life in Prescott, Arizona. The move was a spiritual journey.

I am familiar with hopelessness. Since I was barely twenty years old, I've sought counseling for depression and a lack of self-esteem. My early years were spent as a military child. I was born to a father who had problems with alcohol and a mother who was coping with them. This must have contributed to the sense of uncertainty I felt, as if danger were lurking in the background of every beautiful relationship or situation.

In retrospect, I realize that much of the writing about my early life has dealt with darkness and light. The first significant pieces are from my family's time in Fairbanks, Alaska, in the early 1950's. This was, of course, during the Cold War. The winters of 1951 and 1952 seemed endless. Had I been an adult, I might have thought of Sartre's *No Exit*, in which the characters come to realize that they are trapped for eternity with one another, in a hotel that is hell. Although I was only four and five years old, the memories remain crisp and clear, like the frigid air I breathed through my scarf mask as I walked through the streets.

I rode the bus to the Little Red Schoolhouse for kindergarten. In the morning it was still dark, and the stars were out. I would lean my head against the frosted window to watch the northern lights shimmering across the sky.

1. www.darknightofthesoul.org

The Little Red Schoolhouse was a warm, bright place to be during the day, but the darkness waited for me outside. After school, I hurriedly climbed back onto the bus to go home. I was always happy to see Mom standing at the bus stop by our brick apartment building. She would be waiting in her brown mukluks and long, furry coat with a hood.

Darkness invaded the underground tunnels, too. They looped around like an endless maze. Other kids roller-skated in the tunnels, but I was afraid even to walk to my friends' apartments. I feared getting lost, because the tunnels all looked alike. My heart would jolt if I heard a footstep or the whining of roller skates coming around a curve.

Tommy was one of the friends I dared walk through the tunnels to visit. I liked to play with him, because he made me feel less alone. When his family was transferred back to the States—at the time, Alaska was a territory—their plane crashed, and the whole family died.

"What is it like to be dead?" I thought.

At four and five years old, I had no notion about the strategic importance of Alaska to our country's Cold War strategy. Only a three-mile stretch separated the closest points of Russia's Big Diomede Island and Alaska's Little Diomede Island. The Cold War climate and the nuclear arms race strengthened what people on both sides called the "Ice Curtain" between the two countries. Ladd Air Force Base, the very place where I lived, where I traveled through tunnels to visit friends, and where I went to school in the dark, was an important American base for reconnaissance of

Russian military activity. From Ladd, SAC aircraft missions were launched to collect information about the Soviets through electronic surveillance. We were on one of the northernmost surveillance sites, a "front line," so to speak. The base's function was to identify and destroy any attackers headed farther south. This made us fodder for war.

I understand now the importance of our location, but as a small child, the only clues I had were my dad's secretive exits during the night.

I'm tucked into bed. I'm warm, though the chill of the Alaska night seeps through the edges of the windows next to me. I'm asleep when a loud siren blasts the quiet like a battle horn. I hear murmuring, movement through our apartment, and then the door closes firmly. Daddy is gone again into the night. This is called an alert, and he has no choice but to go. Something must be happening with the Russians.

"When your dad is called away like this, he doesn't know where he is going or when he'll come back. He might have to go somewhere secret and do an important job," Mom tells me each time he leaves in the night. I lie in my warm bed and wish he had kissed me goodbye before he left.

During the high alerts, particularly in the months of light, we were warned not to look out of our windows. We were supposed to close all of the curtains and stay away from them. Our apartment was in the basement.

One day, against the rules, I climbed onto a chair and peeked out of our ground-level window. Soldiers in helmets and uniforms were doing maneuvers, with their rifles in hand. They seemed to be playing hide-and-seek around some tall fir trees. It was fun to watch, but, like the siren in the night, these maneuvers left me with a feeling that things were not safe. Many nights I woke up to the darkness and total silence. I would wait to hear the siren until I fell asleep again, hoping that Daddy wouldn't have to leave.

A photo taken during this time in Alaska speaks to my experience there. My sister, Marge, took it right after we had viewed a huge bear at the University of Alaska Museum. To me, this bear looked twenty feet tall, but Marge said he was only nine. Gazing up at him, I became invisible. Minutes later, in the photo, I am alone in an empty field, somewhere on the university campus. Marge is far away from me. I look so tiny that you can't see my face. It's like a vague smudge on top of my body. If I am smiling, you can't tell it. No one else is around.

Scattered relationships and multiple marriages put me in counseling throughout graduate school and my professional life as a college teacher. I had finally found the right marital partner, when, a few years later, it was time for my son to move out. He was an only child from an earlier marriage. My husband, Roger, and I decided to leave the area and move to Prescott. It was then that I encountered the most devastating darkness of my life. Our decision to move away from my son, friends, and a twenty-three-year teaching job in Michigan was enough to throw me into a dark despair.

This was my "long good-bye."

Roger and I knew we would be leaving for a full year before it actually happened. We had already purchased a home in Prescott. During this time I tried to maintain a sense of continuity in my job. I taught my classes and worked overtime with the honors students. Like the military kid who was always expecting the next move, I was on hold. I was temporary. Everyone knew we were leaving.

In late October we sold the house I had purchased ten years earlier, for my son and myself. Roger drove to Arizona to meet the movers there and unload our furniture. He would be gone for at least two weeks. I stayed behind, living in a lovely, furnished house owned by some friends, and worked. We had until the next May before we would leave for good.

Limbo. It was then that I entered soul darkness.

On a Friday night there was an eclipse of the moon. I had forced myself to go out to the local bookstore, to be amongst people, lights, and conversation. It didn't help. The voices around me were cacophony. Like the clatter of sound at a county fair. Empty noise.

They think they have reasons to live. They act as if what they were doing makes sense, has importance. But I know better. I know it is all an absurdity, a long waiting for nothing. Everywhere I look there is darkness. Now I understand purgatory.

I sat on a chair in the psychology section, near the crowded coffee shop. I read about how people take their lives and the signs that precede their suicides.

My cell phone rang. It was my son, Owen. I asked him to join me at the bookstore. When he arrived, he stared at me. I could tell that he saw my emptiness. We returned to the rented house together.

Owen seemed to know that I was in a bad place. He lingered with me until almost 1:00 a.m. He talked on about his life, his hopes for purchasing houses on the southwest side of Detroit. He said he would renovate buildings and rent them to low-income families. He would contribute to the community, to the resuscitation of Detroit. He would clean up the neighborhood. He would get rid of the drug dealers. He would be a responsible citizen. These were his dreams.

After Owen left that night, I knew I had to keep going, if for no other reason than that I could not set an example of defeat and despair for him. He was so full of hope. I would make myself get out of bed. I would try to focus on my work. I would read, and I would write poems, even if they were about sadness and emptiness. My niece Terry had given me a picture frame with sepia photos of a nineteenth century family lacquered around its edges. The bottom of the frame admonished me, "Remember What Is Important."

What kind of picture could I possible put in this frame? How can I pretend to care when nothing matters?

My poem "Picture Frame" expresses this emptiness.

Serious faces,
even the children do not smile.
They search for their center,
a blank white space, empty,
cuts off half a face on the right,
a body at the top.

There is no center. It might as
well be black, bottomless, might
as well devour the viewer
who seeks to understand these

people, this family, its history
tied to a dark thread, a river of
despair that bleeds its way from
one generation to the next.

The picture I will place in this frame
will be dim and unknown,
dark, paralyzed, meaningless,
loveless.
The picture I will place in this frame
will complete the family photo album,
sad faces,

        children who cannot smile.

The idea of family legacy seems absurd. All a game to pretend that I want to preserve something important. What is important about voices of the dead? All of the lost ones who have died? My sister, Marge, Mom, and Dad are all dead.
    What's the point?
    When Roger heard my voice on the phone the night of the eclipse, he cut his trip short. He cancelled his plans to work on our Arizona house and made a plane reservation to come back to Detroit. He had longed to see the mountains and the sunlight, yet he returned to the winter darkness that was smothering me.

This was the coldest winter in my memory. It set in at zero degrees and hovered there, moving up to eight or ten degrees in the daytime, then back down to below zero.

I can't remember the sunshine glinting off of Mingus Mountain in Prescott from the full-length windows of our new home. I've lost the colors of the double rainbow that shone after a summer monsoon last August, and the red liquid drunk by the hummingbird on the deck. I've lost the light of the planets glittering in a sky of black velvet that made me think tomorrow could hold hope, energy, life, and strength, even under the unrelenting blanket of darkness that is Michigan in winter. It is gone, this lighted place.

January 2004. The long goodbye stretches out—endless and dark—with the coldest of winters. Muted light. No clarity. I am suspended, muddled.

February 2004. There has been a terrible accident. My friend Sharon's son Eliot is dead. I could hardly hear her on the phone this Monday morning. I heard only the weeping in her voice, the strain of trying to speak the unspeakable—that her oldest son is dead. Hit by a train last night, in the dark. He was on foot. He tried to jump away, the engineer said. Eliot. A gifted musician who could play anything on the piano by age twelve. Eliot, who had sung in a boy's voice, still sweetly soprano, at his grandfather's funeral, and who had played the organ only a year ago at his mother's remarriage.

This is a mother's greatest fear. I am afraid to look at Sharon's grief, to embrace it. I know that if my son died, I would no longer want to live. I watch her going on with her days, riding over waves of pain.

At Eliot's funeral, I see my son enter the sanctuary of the Catholic Church. I am unable to stop crying. I fear Owen's death, even while he kneels to pray next to me, before the funeral Mass begins. He wears a hound's tooth jacket, black and white in pattern, with a yellow tie as a carefully chosen accent.

He rises, and we embrace. I cry as if I have lost him already. He doesn't seem to mind that I have smeared his cheek with my tears. He holds me with his strong grip. He accepts my grief, my fear about him. He reassures me that he will think before he acts. This time, I believe him. This time, I am calmed by the man he has become. One who will look both ways, he assures me.

He is managing his life. I know that he will embrace his passions. He will not starve or lack medical care. He will find his way in business. He will move with confidence and understanding. He will prosper.

Why is this winter so dark?

I have lived through twenty-five Michigan winters. I have loved the winters here. I have loved the crisp air, the beauty of snow unsullied by city pollution. I have enjoyed walks in the cold afternoons. I have watched the world turn through cycle after cycle.

But now, this winter darkness is like an animal of prey. The lighting is muted inside our rented house, and sparse light comes through the snow clouds. The cold penetrates my heart like sharp icicle needles. There is no escape.

At work, I can't understand the voices that surround me in the hallways. I am walking in another realm, detached from the business and clutter of classes and meetings and students.

Deadening cold sets in and promises to freeze what little life remains. Everything grinds slowly to a halt. All turn inward, seeking even the darkness for comfort, as if the darkness offered warmth.

February is the shortest month, this month of Eliot's death.

In March, light begins to return. I emerge with it. Late at night, and in the early morning hours, I read *The Gospel of Mary Magdalene*. Traditional theology is set aside for a powerful message of hope. "All that is born, all that is created, all the elements of nature are interwoven and united with each other. All that is composed shall be decomposed; everything returns to the origins of matter."

I recognize ideas that I had discovered in Native American belief and in my graduate studies of Transcendentalism. I am a part of the whole. This makes soul sense to me.

As I mull over the text, highlighting passages that jump out at me, I recall the fundamentalist teachings of my Protestant upbringing. I remember the guilt and self-loathing. I was an unhealthy religious zealot as a teenager. Now, I have discovered words from this ancient document, Mary Magdalene's words, which bring me to a place of peace.

"Attachment to matter
gives rise to passion against nature.
Thus trouble arises in the whole body;
this is why I tell you:
Be in harmony…

If you are out of balance,
take inspiration from manifestations
of your true nature.
Those who have ears,
let them hear.

Peace be with you—may my Peace
arise and be fulfilled within you!
Be vigilant, and allow no one to mislead you
by saying:
'Here it is!' or
'There it is!'
For it is within you
that the Son of Man dwells.
Go to him,
for those who seek him, find him.
Walk forth,
and announce the gospel of the Kingdom.

For it is within you
that the Son of Man dwells."[2]

---

2. *The Gospel of Mary Magdalene* translated by Jean-Yves Leloup, Inner Traditions, Rochester, VT 05676
© 1997, 2002 Inner Traditions/Bear&Co

I envision myself gazing at the mountains that surround Prescott. I think about my son. I will miss him.

"We can talk every day, Mom," he says.

I know that I will be happier in that place where light can find its way into the crevices of my darkened spirit. Light is everywhere in Arizona. Even after the sun sets, the stars are out, and there is light.

One night, I awaken, visit our deck, and write "A Rumble of Hunger."

4:09 a.m. August. Clear night for stars.
I awaken with a rumble of emptiness.
I want to see the darkness, hear the silence
of the night. The deck is quiet. Only
distant sounds of roaring trucks puncture
a velvet blanket of night, stars like scattered
dust, stars I cannot see in the city.
Orion journeys toward fall, his time of awakening.
Tonight, still, he lingers for what is left
of his summer rest.

The canvas of stars offers refuge,
company in the emptiness that
awoke me.

I could stay here all night.
I could drink the stars,
their sweetness,
until I am drunk with beauty.

Yes, I tell myself, the light will be there, in the mountains of Arizona.

2007. It is three years since we arrived at our new home, three years since this time of the long goodbye. In the morning I awaken to see the sunrise through the window that faces our bed. Sunrises here are full of light and color, pinks and purples and blues. It's summer now, and Roger has put out a new feeder for the hummingbirds. We have tomatoes, herbs, peppers, and pansies planted in pots on the deck. On the mountain that is our side yard, we are nurturing the irises planted by the last owner. They come up sporadically amongst the rocks and cacti and bushes. In some spots we have planted gladiola bulbs for the fall. Their blooming is something to look forward to.

Owen has married. He and his wife Sandra have a little girl, Camila, born in late spring, two years ago. Another child is on the way. They have visited us for the first time in our new home. After returning to Detroit, Owen says he misses the radiance, the color, and the warmth of our place. He wants to move to the Southwest as soon as possible. He too will seek the light.

Rick Kempa

Something You've Done

Think of it as a rock
you kicked from its place
on your walk, something

you can pick up, inspect—
the chips and bumps,
the dark, coarse grain,
the purple thread of quartz.
A mass, a shape you
close your fist around,
squeeze, put down.

M. L. Cordle

The Locust Tree

On the very crest of a hill, standing alone, was once an unspectacular locust tree. I'd never noticed this tree until after it was struck by lightning, around the time I was entering adolescence. I remember the moment when I first saw it. One charred branch had splintered from the torso. It looked like an old witch's hand splayed upon the barren March ground. The tree captivated me. I had to see it up close. I made the trek up the rugged slope that day, and I returned to the crest of that hill many times over the course of my youth.

I would climb the fallen limb, with its sturdy, leafless fingers, to perch upon the tree. From its branches, I sailed ships. I launched rockets and dreams. I pined for a boy, nursed a broken heart, then pined for another boy. I thought about my soul. I filled my lungs with Appalachian air, and I ached for what I would be one day.

This was a poignant place—the branches of the locust tree up on top of the hill. We were two of a kind, harboring hope for another summer.

I was in need of spiritual mending. This tree became my refuge, my higher plane. It was my connection to all things hoped for but not seen.

Yet, in time, the prayers I sent out as a girl were forgotten. The questions I had directed at the faceless sky from my broken locust. The answers I had waited for. All were forgotten, as I outgrew the resilience of youth.

After two decades, I rediscovered the locust tree. I returned to that harbinger of hope, the connection to my dreams. I struggled up onto my perch and listened.

My heart was hurting, as it used to when I was a child, impatient to seize the unknown and magnificent. The tangled mass of emotion in my chest clamored to find a rhythm that made sense. What had happened to me? Where had I been, and what had I done that was of any meaning?

After a while, I climbed down from this tree, a skeletal testimony to some long-past storm. Although I'd put my whole being into listening, I had heard nothing. Although I had been so high up on this hill, and so high up in the locust, that I might have heard the girlish voice of my lost youth, I had heard only the sound of my weary, bumbling heart.

I had witnessed the mountains, my heritage, spread out around me like a silly quilt, and understood nothing. I felt only the pulse of my own sadness and the thrum of my grieving blood. It was as though the weight of years had stacked up against me. My lungs struggled to expand beneath the pressure of age.

Worst of all, I thought, the importance of this place had diminished, along with everything else that made up my life. In a last ode to childhood, I stood back and gazed at this friend from the past. It was then that I was shocked to see that the locust was dying.

From all angles save this one, my locust had appeared unchanged. It had seemed a tree like any other. A tree that November had stripped of its leaves. Yet, I had misunderstood the long-past storm whose tentacle of awesome and terrible white light had pierced the locust. In the years that had toiled by, I had not known what transformation was taking place deep within the tree. Within the fissure, born from that jagged strike of lightning, lay my ignorance. I had seen the severed branch, but not the damage that would destroy the locust.

The tree had been a rugged pillar of strength. Now, it was a hollow shell. I stepped into its weathered core, the silence of this still and precious memory, and touched the parched wood.

I scratched my initials into the trunk. Its smooth, dry surface had once been the pulpy core of a young tree. Although inner beauty clings tenaciously to the heart, the heart's days are fleeting.

My feet sank against the fertile soil. The wind whistled through a crevice in the fractured bark. I breathed it. I listened. Was this sound the wind or a whisper from the place of all that is hoped for but not seen?

I mourned my loss.

What I beheld quite suddenly, however, was life.

Although most of the locust's leaves had been scattered by Autumn, a few still clung to the branches. These branches had not been shorn off in the storm of my youth. My tree had tasted last summer as surely as I had.

Nothing was left of her but a shell; the tree was cracked open from bower to base. Yet leaves—tender, golden, and vibrant with a faith that had lasted for ages—bespoke a life that was no less glorious than those dream-laden ships I had set to sail from her helm, while still young and bold enough to believe.

I stood within a living thing. At last, I understood.

I too had endured storms and striking lightning over the course of my life. They had weakened me, an average soul. Until now. Like the locust tree, I stood by faith alone.

Corrine De Winter

Statues of Sekhmet

We move through the ancient
Temple of Dundar,
Pass seven venerable statues
Beside the dark water.
I have come to a place of virgins
Caught in plaster,
Some without hands.

It seems as though the hands,
Held out or up to welcome
The Holy Spirit,
Are the first to break
Against time.
Yet, next to the eyes—
All they have seen—
It is the hands
Which have held
Love and suffering,
The hands

That have lent warmth
Or offered sustenance.

These virgins sitting
With no mission
In a busy room
Beckon prayer.
I am hesitant to pass
Without listening
To their stories,
Without holding my
Palms outward,
As one earthbound
Waiting to receive grace.

Deborah DeNicola

Moment

The air was more presence
than space
in the oval window's dusk.

There were no contradictions
in the dimensions of the ceiling,
no need

to wrap the room's perimeter
around my shoulder. No perimeter
at all—rhythmic
cognition of the here and now
on earth. A white spider

crawled across the quilt.
Her pilgrimage, a garnet
square to blue.

It was time to weave
within the paradox, whose

cadence met my eyes
upon opening, my

eyes in synch
inside
the mind's unbidden

whisper: *See,*
all is new.[3]

Wendy Brown

Choices

This is what I want:
    To hold your hand in the terrible
    silence between life and death.
    Not to say choose me but to say,

---

3. *The Book of Revelation* 21:5

Choose!
Choose life and be strong, you who
     are the fury in my wind.
Choose to be tender, you who
     are the glimmer in my clouded hope.

Because of you, I write words.
     I am as loyal as my supermarket pen
     and as fickle as a rusted sword.

Will I hold your hand during
the time of false alarm? Do you
paint my sadness with the color
of flame? Am I so
transparent that you must
trace a line from my tongue
to my bones? Maybe I also
want forest, a damp
shade, a nested meadow,
and a lark to sing.

Yes, I own nothing but dried
roses, and you do not know
how they bloomed in the cool

autumn of a young girl
come back to life after the
poisoned apple failed.

I hold onto all I ever imagined:
      Our fine skins of pearl,
      our sharp cluster of sins,
      our warmth seeping into the sun,

thrown to the gods like scraps
      to appease the wolf-hunger,
thrown to the Spirit who catches
      us like pollen in her bejeweled hair.

Laura Gallagher

Chapter Eight: In Which the World Implodes

The world collapsed last night in a dream.
A man with a thick, twisted-yarn mustache and
stringy white hair explained the situation:
We have only hours. There's no way around it, and
did I not explain that there will be an explosion?

The people around me looked uncomfortable,
sitting on those scratchy carpet chairs they have
at roller rinks, wondering how to spend their eleventh hour
and fifty-eighth minute—
beneath a stranger, beside a loved one, or quiet
under the eyes of the ender of
eternity.

In other dreams, Satan has unrolled his long vermilion
tongue to throw knives at me in my kitchen, his red,
painted face leering at me, trout-like eyes laughing, rolling.
There is panic. Screaming.
I can't catch my breath,

find the door, move my
legs.

But, no. The end of the world was quite calm.
I walked to the picture window, and stared at
our ineffable host. He winked at me as the window
turned blue like a broken television and everything—stopped
no
froze.
I awoke.

I opened my eyes and
looked at you.

Did you know darling, now everything is different.

J. Roman

How Can You Say There's a God?

How can you say there's a God?
How can you say there's a heaven in the sky?

Tell me,
tell me something I can believe.
Tell me something that makes me believe
there's something bigger than me.

Tell me,
what did we do to the Son of God?

The same thing we do today.
Kill.

Tell me something I can believe.
Death.
There's something I can see.
There's something I believe.

God left.
Haven't you seen?

Haven't you seen how we live?
Can't you see the suffering of our kids?

Oh! You live in the pretty house, guarded
by men with heavy guns.
You say,
"Don't get close.
You will die.
Don't talk about the truth,
because you will die."

Sure, you don't see our suffering.
You're the ones who supply it.
Now you judge me!

Eyes
already on me,
sizing me up.

My eyes
reveal nothing.

Judging me?
I'm judged the gatekeeper of hell.
My back
pocket hiding the stash.

Crack cocaine.
Heroin.
My name?
You don't want to know.

Feel my hatred rise.
Addict or dealer,
who's worse?
The one who wants or the one who supplies?

What about the rich,
the rich
that get rich from their laws.

What about the rest?
We,
the poor, who experience
racism. Poverty.
Society.

Everybody wants money.
We are all part of the chain.
Giving it or taking it.

Eyes
naive to my
wisdom?
Surprise.

Hell holds too many bodies.
Poor ventilation.
Ubiquitous smell.
Souls burning.
Poison to hypnotize the brain.
With a single touch,
dissolve to dust.
Rats hunt for food.
Dim light shows the end of the hall.
Dirty window.
Rusted breath.
My fingertips touch the gate.

Tell me, where is your God?
Because I can't find mine.

Does he love me as he loves you?
If he does,
why are we not in the same place?
Why do you see blue sky, and I see grey?
Why are kids being raped, hurt, and killed?
Do they have to be angels to be protected?
Or are the innocent there to be killed?
Because that's what I see. Every day.

That's what's happening to them. Every day.
Fathers raping their own daughters.
Mothers killing their own babies.
Doctors calling themselves doctors just to vindicate
the killing of an unborn child.
Police call themselves "The Law"
to point their guns at skin that is not their color.

Tell me, where is your God?
Tell me,
so I can go find him.
Tell me if I'm worthy to see the sky.
Tell me if I'm worthy to live this life.
Because I feel like I'm going to die.

Now,
Tell me, where is God?
Tell me who he is.
Tell me.
Please.

J. Roman

My Best Friend in Jail Is Gay

Let me start by saying that no, I'm not gay. And yes, I am a prisoner in the State of New York, with a friend that is gay.

I'm writing about someone who's real cool with me. He (oops) She is my friend. I don't judge him. Our friendship is based on respect. Her name (Yes, I have to call him by "her.") is Vanessa.

Let me tell you how I met Vanessa. It was December of 2001. I had already been in jail for almost a year. At the city jail on Rikers Island.

I was at the intake cell—"reception" to those of us coming from court. I was chilling with sixty or more of the craziest criminals. A few were coming from court, just like me. Others were fresh from the streets.

You could see the difference between the ones who'd been in jail for a while and those who had just come in.

I'd been pretty clean for almost a year. Not doing drugs much. Not drinking. Not getting laid. Sleeping better. I was big and red. Healthier than when I got locked up.

The ones coming in from the streets still had a dope habit. They were dirty and smelly. Their skin looked yellow. They had filthy hair and huge eyes that might have been pretty once. Now, their eyes were bloodshot and smudged black with fatigue.

I was feeling like I was lost in a lost world. I saw their hunger. I thought back, wondering if I'd looked like that when I'd come in.

If you were to peer into that cell of sixty-plus inmates, you'd see what I'm talking about. It was like the inside of a can of Vienna sausage. There were men soiling themselves. They couldn't hold their sickness. Others were sleeping on the floor or pacing back and forth. More were smoking and talking crap about their war stories. Looking at them, I was sure they hadn't killed a cockroach. It was a whole different world.

I was standing in the corner with my boy Satana. He was an old timer. He had gone home after doing fifteen years in jail. Five months hadn't passed before he was back. It had been a drug sell to an undercover cop.

We were in a corner of the cell. Smoking. Satana was down with the Latin Kings. He was an old guy, but he had juice. There were other Kings around him. Always giving him things. Drugs. Cigarettes. Making phone calls for him. He was one of the heads.

We were always talking. When I wasn't with him, I would be alone. I didn't like talking to anyone else.

Satana was there when I got into my first fight on Rikers, with Tyson. Tyson looked like he ate people. He was big.

It was my first day in jail. After a day and night at intake, I'd been sent to C-95, Dormitory 2L. It's called "The Project."

It was 7:30 in the morning. Time for breakfast. I'd taken my tray and sat down at the first table I'd seen. What I didn't know was that I'd sat in the wrong area.

This guy the size of a refrigerator tells me to get out of his seat. And to leave my tray. His eyes were on me. He was looking at me with those eyes. Drilling into my soul. Seeking out my weakness.

I'm not going to lie. I was scared. I wasn't scared of him, but I was scared. Anyone who knows what I'm talking about knows what I mean.

I stood up, looking down at the table, and without hesitation, I picked up my tray and hit him in the head. We started to fight. He got me good with a few punches, but I got the last hit. With the tray.

The officers came over to the table. I was lucky, because the female officer took my side. She wrote on the ticket that Tyson was always abusing other inmates. After that day, I never saw him again. His seat became mine.

Satana asked me who I was riding with. I knew what he was talking about, but I pretended I didn't

"You a King?"

"No," I said. "I'm from the Island. Puerto Rico."

He guessed I was about twenty-five.

Still, I told him nothing about myself. After that day, we became good friends.

So, we were at intake. We had just come from court. The corrections officer from the front table called Satana to go back to his unit. We said our goodbyes.

I stood alone in the corner. I was smoking a cigarette and thinking about my case. A crew of inmates came into the cell. I looked to see what all the commotion was about. That's when I saw her. Vanessa.

At first, I thought she was a nurse checking on one of the inmates who was lying on the floor. Sometimes they send someone in to do that. When the corrections officer closed the metal door, it hit me. This woman wasn't a nurse. She was one of us. A prisoner.

If you saw Vanessa, you wouldn't know that she was a he. He looks like a she. She has white skin. Not rough like a man's. She has long black hair, not like a man's. Her face and body are petite, not like a man's. There isn't a thing you can see in her that tells you she is a man.

She sat down in a corner. It was like she was famous. She had a few of her girls with her. None of them compared with her. The bunch of them looked like men pretending to be girls.

I could see some of the other men looking, ready to hunt down their prey. There were inmates giving cigarettes and marijuana to Vanessa. You know. Being nice and all, because in hell, she was a woman. Men doing a lot of time would do anything to get a piece of that cherry pie.

I'm not going to lie. I saw a woman. I did. Still, my mind was saying, "She is a man." I couldn't imagine myself with someone like her. Her looks didn't matter.

Every time I went to court, it was the same routine. Come back and sit for four or five hours at intake until the corrections officers were ready to send me to my unit. By now, I had moved up, from a dorm to a cell. It was more private.

I hated to go to court, because I never received good news. The D.A. was offering twenty years for a robbery and an attempted murder. I used to come back from court sick, thinking how old I would be when I finished my twenty years in hell.

Every time I came back from court, Vanessa was there too. She was going to a different court. To one in Queens.

One day, I was smoking a cigarette. I was thinking hard. I knew I wouldn't be going home for a long time. I heard a voice asking for a light, taking me out of my own crazy world. I gave her a look.

She looked back at me. "I'm sorry," she said and started to walk away.

The look I'd given her was a look that said, "Touch me again, and I'll kill you." Then, I mellowed. She was just asking for a light. And, after all, it was Vanessa.

I said, "Hey, here."

She said, "I'm sorry to bother you."

I gave her my lighter and said, "It's cool."

There weren't a lot of inmates at intake this time around. We were fifteen at the most. She sat a few feet from me. She was complaining about how long it took the corrections officers to take us back to the unit. Still, I wasn't talking to her. I didn't want her, or anyone else, to get confused.

While I listened, I remembered that my aunt always said, "Don't judge people by their looks."

My aunt was more man than any other man. She took responsibility for things. She raised my sister and me when our mother was running crazy in the streets with drugs. My aunt was always with us. Her family was our family.

From the day she took me in, my aunt told me, "Don't look at a person for what they've done. Look at a person for how he or she is with you." From that day, I learned to see people for what we are. Human beings with feelings.

But I was in jail now. I was in a different world. I couldn't look at Vanessa for what she was. Still, I didn't act like I was a gangster, or like I wanted nothing to do with her.

She was always there at intake when I came back from court.

I'd say, "Hi."

She'd say, "Hi back."

After a few weeks passed, Vanessa moved onto my unit. She moved into the cell next to mine. (When the Department of Corrections is going to move an inmate, they don't care who they move. If there's an opening, they will move anyone, without caring whether you want that person next to you or not. In jail, you have to live with your enemy next to you. That's how it is.)

"Hi," she said.

"Hi back."

I gave Vanessa 7:00 p.m. for the shower. That was her time. After 7:00 p.m., she couldn't be in the bathroom, unless she had to. You know what I mean.

My crew were the ones running this unit. There were units Latinos couldn't live in because the Bloods would beat them up, just as there were units the Bloods couldn't live in because the Latinos would do the same. The whites liked to live with us Latinos for different reasons. The truth was, everything was messed up. Blacks hitting whites. Latinos hitting blacks. That's jail. All messed up.

Vanessa and I started to talk at night. She from her cell. Me from mine.

Little by little, we talked about our families. Then, she began to tell me about her love affairs with other inmates. Secrets. Who was who.

She told me about a member of the Rat Hunters. He was big, tall, and married. He was always talking about how he was hitting this and doing that. He acted like a killer. But a killer who liked it with her, she said.

She had men giving her weed, coke, and heroin. There were inmates buying her sneakers. It was crazy. I couldn't believe what men would do for her. But that's jail. Crazy.

One night, she called me from her cell. I leaned close to the edge of mine. I couldn't see her face.

"What?" I said.

"Here."

"What's that?" I asked.

"It's a smoke."

We talked all night. That became our routine. She liked to drink coffee. I would bring it for her, with lots of cream and sugar. We were living large.

Then I got sentenced to nine years.

I left Rikers Island. I knew I wouldn't see her again. The years passed.

One day, a group of new inmates came to this jail I'm at. One of them called me by name. I didn't hug her or anything, but I was glad to see her. Vanessa.

I was with my boy Black.

Black looked at me and said, "What the…"

I said, "Yeah. He's cool."

"If he's your friend, he must be cool," Black said.

Vanessa had cut her hair. She looked even better. After six years.

"What are you doing here? You back?" she asked.

"No. I'm still here. I never left."

She looked down. "Oh, I thought—"

I interrupted her and said, "What are you doing here? I know this is a new one for you."

"How do you know?"

"Your number." Her number meant she'd been sentenced in 2007.

"I got into trouble, but I'll be gone soon."

"Yeah. What you got?"

"Two flat." She said it with a smile.

"Good," I said.

I wasn't happy to see her in jail, but I was happy to see her again. We were always talking. Spending time with her felt like talking to one of my best girlfriends. I told her that I don't smoke anymore. Not in jail, or at all. I was writing and doing better for myself.

She too was at a different stage in her life. She was getting married. The guy was in his forties. He was a millionaire. He wanted to pay for an operation for her to become a woman. The way she told me about it, I knew she wasn't comfortable with the idea.

"That's what you want? To be all woman?" I asked her.

I had never seen Vanessa like this. She started to cry. Not out loud like we men do, but in a soft, gentle way. Like a girl, when someone has broken her heart. She told me why.

When her brother Remy got killed, he didn't have any kids. One night, Vanessa had gone to see her parents. She hadn't seen them for weeks.

She'd opened the door quietly to surprise her mother. Then, she'd heard her father talking.

"Now that Remy is dead, I'll die without a grandchild. My only hope for a grandchild is dead."

Vanessa had stood, listening by the door. She'd left without letting her parents know she'd been there.

As she told her story, I forgot where I was. It didn't matter to me how the other inmates saw me, because I knew who I was. And I knew who she was. I put my hand on her shoulder, letting her know that I felt her pain.

Black was standing a few feet from where we were. Listening.

Vanessa's time passed. Again, we said goodbye. She told me she would write to me. I told her not to send me anything. I was cool. I told her to take care and not to come back. For the first time, I hugged her like a friend.

She hugged me back and told me, "It would be nice if more people were like you. You don't judge me. You're a real man."

We laughed.

"You're an angel in hell," she said.

I'd never seen myself the way she did. Maybe it was true. I was in a program, talking with kids from school. A counselor would bring in students who were starting to get into trouble with the law. We inmates would tell them about how life was in jail. And I was always helping the young kids who were in jail for the first time. Telling them to get their G.E.D.

I thank Vanessa for making me a better person.

Six or seven months had passed since she'd left. I hadn't heard from her. I didn't know if she was alive or dead.

It was Saturday morning. Saturdays in jail are dead. For inmates who get visitors, it's the best day. But inmates like me, who don't get a visit, don't want to get up until after visiting's over.

I was sleeping when an officer called me. "Roman, you have a visit."

"Are you sure it's me?" I said.

I knew it couldn't be for me, because my family's in Orlando, Florida. Plus, my little sister—when she comes to New York, she'd rather visit her friends than her brother in jail.

I stood in front of the officer. I wasn't sure what to do.

The officer saw the look on my face. He could be the nastiest officer out of all of them, but that morning, he was cool.

He said, "Roman, go down. If you see it isn't for you, come back up."

I got dressed. I went down. The officer from the visiting room took my name and numbers.

I asked him, "Do you know the name of the person who's here to visit me?" I thought it might be my mother. I hadn't seen her for a few years.

He told me that he didn't have her name.

Her name, I said to myself. Her. Maybe my ex? Nah, she still hates my guts.

My heart was pumping. I was curious, but at the same time, I was scared. For the first time in a long time, I was afraid of something.

I could see a crowd of people sitting at the tables as I walked down the hallway. Still, I didn't recognize any of the faces. I went back to the officer sitting at the desk. I told him that someone had made a mistake.

He looked at me like I was nothing. "What is your name?" he asked.

"Roman. 02A3568."

He looked down at his notebook. "Line C. Table 4."

I turned around again. I counted the lines, then the tables. From what I saw, it couldn't be for me. I counted again. First the lines, then the tables. Just to be sure.

I looked back at the officer. From the look on his face, I knew it was better not to ask him any more questions.

I walked over to the table. I felt hypnotized. She was beauty at its best. Long, black hair hung halfway down her back. Her skin was white, but I could tell she was Latina. As I got closer, she turned her head towards me. It was then that I could see her whole face.

She was beautiful for real. Perfect lips. Perfect eyes. Perfect everything. But still, I knew she wasn't there for me.

I got to the table. Before she said a word, I said, "Excuse me, but I think you have the wrong name. I'm sorry, but I'm not the Roman you're looking for."

She smiled. "She called you Bol, right?"

"Yeah. But I don't know you."

"Sit down," she said. "I'm Vanessa's cousin."

I shook my head to clear it. "Oh, how's she doing?"

"She's fine. I'm Angelica."

Yes, indeed. She was an angel. She was beautiful. She is beautiful.

"Vanessa sent me to thank you," she said. She told me that Vanessa always talked about me and what a man I was. That's why Angelica had come to see me. She wanted to see if I was real.

My point in telling the story is this. See people for what they are.

I don't care anymore about color or race. I don't care if he wants to be a she. If I judge someone today, maybe, tomorrow, my kid will be just like the person I judged, the person I mistreated. Let a person be happy with this life.

See people for what they are. Human.

Fredrick Zydek

Praying When No One Is Watching

I have nothing against corporate prayer
or even those recited as sound bytes
in polite and popular religious places.
A sense of belonging to the universe,

knowing magic words that subdue it,
and being part of a clan that owns them
is potent stuff that gladdens the journey.
But when you step into prayer on your own,

it can be as scary as the moment you will
take your last breath and slip alone into
the great mystery that awaits us all. Still,
praying alone has its own rewards.

Ease yourself into the silence that wants
to surround you. Listen to it the way you
once hoped you would listen to the future.
Dream out loud. Celebrate all the questions

vying for your attention. One by one they
will take their proper places. Eventually things
that have been nesting in prayer long before
you arrived will find sure ways to guide you.

Bill Roberts

My Advice to You

My advice to you,
If you insist on
Asking for advice,
Is this:

Take a peek at
The potential
Advice-giver's resume
First.

Be sure
He or she is someone
Worthy of employment.

Oh yes—
Be certain
To check references too.

Everyone these days
Poses as an expert.

You may be wise
To re-think
Even asking for advice.

Barry Ballard

Outside the Herd

The dissenter is every human being at those moments of his life when he resigns momentarily from the herd and thinks for himself.
—Archibald MacLeish

Oh still night, roaring after me like prey
moving under your stars. I am a commoner
in a common herd, bellowing or screeching,
or reveling in my rebellion. Why
is my body a school, why the nightshade
of history a nightshade at all? I swerve
at the poison of complacency, reaching
for the departure of a fountain's light

spilling outside your shadows. Feed on me
at the root, and you'll spit me out. Dreamer
with thorns, I can walk through lightning and find
it dazzling, paint a background over the breed
that sees nothing, and sleep with the leaner
words that need filling, waking with a new mind.

Barry Ballard

Waking

Heave, and a light, a little light, will nimbus your going forth.
—Charles Wright

You're seeing the world with its sharp-angled
shadows, colorless, speaking in your sleep
like an inward prophet with the windowsill's
ashes in his hands. Only cold light weeps,
but the heart tries to swallow it, the stark
refractions, scrambled landscapes, the gleaming
beads of violet transcendence. What part
wakes in the actor's mask of your blinking

shutter? What part breathes the sky's
breath leaking through the blinds? The day itself,
a sacrament: The mundane as sacred
bread; and the opposite of fear
moving you through the truth—that is held
like light in the center of your deep sleep.

Jon Wesick

Anicca
(Impermanence)

Hold on to something you think permanent,
and I will take it away. Revel in wealth,
and I will file a lawsuit. Be proud of your good name,
and I will slander. Spouses leave. Children
move away. Old age dispatches health and beauty.
Fundamentalists burn books. Hackers
scramble databases. Even the stars
will go black when space expands.

Look at the bright side.
Some things don't have to be with you forever:
The extra ten pounds around your middle,
your fear of speaking up in public,
the way you rage at loved ones.

I'll leave you only the present moment.
Do what you will with it.

Richard Alan Bunch

Two Monks

One monk says to another:
"Is time's transparence as joyous
as the look in that solitary heron?"

The second replies:
"Yes, as joyous as that shadow-dawn
I live as borrowed rain."

At that moment they noticed
a bird-of-paradise and knew
without saying a word.

Joe Paddock

Dream: A Song for Birds

In the dream, the inner woman's
voice directed gently: "Sing."

This song then is for all
the twisted and the unfulfilled
whose roots run deep in pain,
whose limbs have yet to green.
May those limbs bud and host
springtime birds
of sweet tomorrow.

May this small song hang
somewhere there in dreamtime,
unknotting that net of aches
that catches life.

And may the little limp
I hide in my walk
discover that,

with song,
there is surely dance.

Denise Thompson-Slaughter

Late Autumn Prayer

Soft God, whisper in my hair tonight,
Before the willows turn,
And chokecherries reach out.

Whisper,
And I'll surrender,
Sinking into you, you to me,
Seeping through my bones and pores.
My heart, singing, will open
Shyly like the new spring snowdrop,
Wildly like a scarlet rose in June.

Katherine West

Mandalas

You are the still point
At the center—
Though you are not still
Though you snow
From east to west and
The invisible moon
Glows through your grainy
White
Lighting the way like an old
Lantern

You are the still point
At the center—
The old pine growing up
From between the rocks
Alone at the edge
Of the hill
A leader without
A tribe

You are the still point
At the center—
You stand with arms
Outstretched
You are the four
Directions
You are the sundial
You are the Stonehenge
Calendar
The ritual
The living
The dead

You are the still point
At the center—
I travel your orbit
Like the moon
I travel with you
I always face you
My dark side
Unknown

You are the vanishing point—
I walk towards you
You move

You are the vanishing point—
Everywhere I look
You vanish

You are the still point
At the center—
On cold mornings
I can touch your
Body
I can hold it close
Wear it
Like a living
Amulet
A living stone

You are the vanishing point—
You go down
With the sun
Like a horse
I must lie

On the earth
To feel your warmth

You are the still point
At the center—
Though you are not still
Though you force
Your breath
From my mouth
Though your heart beats
A strange drum
In my chest

Bob Tremmel

Way Beyond Armageddon

There is a naked man
riding the fast and mighty
Hippo of Pursuit out
of the ruined city
on to the steppes.

LALITAMBA

Ahead of them
a cloud of dust burns
deep vermilion
in the distance, ignited
by setting sun

and all night
they press on as one
while it burns hot, then cold
and white in the xeric
light of the rising moon

and on the third day, columns
of flame and smoke
loom as the naked
man and the Hippo
charge straight through

without thinking
and disappear like drops
of water exploding
in hot oil
or fragments of ash

caught up in the wind
and scattered way
beyond the moon, way
beyond the sun.

Rebecca Lilly

Haiku

1.
The monk's light footsteps
From stone to stone; dust tendrils
Like smoke from pebbles

2.
From a green hilltop
A blue kite arrows up, then
Drops, shadowed by sun

Michael Shannon

August Epiphany

Here is tomorrow,
alone
on an August afternoon.

The heart rests in silence.

Tonight,
a purpose will unveil itself.

I'll be there,
waiting,
under the faint glow of a
summer moon.

You'll see.

You'll go there
and see.

Rick Smith

Ghost Wren

ghost wren
dreaming on a cable
posed
and still
like a shadow
about to dart
in a windless space
flesh and fiber
anticipating
the tension of wound steel
a cello in the night
an ordinary cello
still
in a windless room

Rick Smith

Biloxi

for Sharon West

near Biloxi: a shotgun house
the rains muddy and cold
window frames
slam and shatter
someone steals a boat
paddles east
a dog stranded on a roof
a wren finds a nail under the eaves
the wind
shredding anything that moves
drowns out
all other sound
now:
two wrens on a nail dream
against the storm

Rick Smith

Recovery

I crave the orange.
The sugar
might bring me back to life,
a fierce revisitation
in slow motion
so I can study the game film.
I devour the orange,
ripping at pulp,
salvaging any episodic lucidity.
I have too much to learn
at the blackboard
in a fast falling dusk.
If you lie in a hospital bed
cranked into position
there are fluorescent light,
neat porous squares of
acoustical ceiling tile,
the curved track of the modesty curtain.
Here, there is no private dying.

Every stirring clears that linen barrier.
Final shakings and rattlings find ways.
In some distant tree,
the jarring squawk of blue jays
rings with hope.
I'm like a rootball
seeking chutes, tendrils, or
any sprinkling of real light.
I travel where underbrush is expectant.
The poems, when they come,
cover what came before,
and they shine before they are covered themselves.
Rotation of crops fuels innocence,
makes topsoil black with promise.
They say that once I understand
that certain things whispered in the background
give power, I could reach a new plateau.
I listen: Carts on wheels, soap opera
and storm warnings, the way
nursing shoes squeak. And I listen
past these dense cinder blocks, to
traffic, to the racket of the jays,
and to the very breath
of this building, refrigeration,

the modal hum of air conduction,
until I am still and breathless
as any lizard.

I see terra cotta
holding aloe vera and chamomile.
There is sun on the veranda.
My wife is making bread,
and morning is all I know.

Paul Hostovsky

Sharing the Orange

First I hold it out to you
in my hands which are
trembling a little so you
take them in your hands
you take the orange in my
hands in your hands and you
stop my trembling first
then you kiss me with your

eyes wide open and I feel your
hands on the orange and I
hear the skin tear open
I hear your fingernail tear it
ripping it back without taking
your eyes away from my eyes
all this you do without looking
you guide my finger to the wound
and you press my finger into it
and together we peel the rest of it
completely away without looking
away from each other's eyes the wet
soft creature of the orange sitting
naked in our hands the smell of it
rising like a sunrise on our fingers
which we hold up to our noses
and put into each other's mouths
sharing the orange without eating it
tasting the orange without eating it
without looking and without looking away

Janet McCann

Old Family Reels

It's Christmas Eve, and I have Mass to attend,
desserts to prepare, and a few dozen presents to wrap;
old Christmas flashes through my mind like a movie,

how it was a mystery, not Santa Claus but the whole
myth of the thing, its glistening energy, the long
afternoons passed looking for the perfect gift and then

in the end, buying everything in the store, spending
every penny, because it was Christmas, and if you didn't
have someone on the list to give everything to

you could wrap it up and take it to the church,
and you bought it because it was there and it glittered
or it was blue. This was before credit, and anyway,

you were too young. Everything you spent, you had
in your pocket. The dimes, bright silver, and
the heavy nickels and pennies. You had to make sure

nothing was left over. No nickel for a Coke or a big thick
candy bar, because this was Christmas, the season of giving,
and if you got gifts you did not want, that was ok because

of the spirit: Aunt Amy had spent long afternoons embroidering
that undershirt and, while you weren't about to actually
wear it, you could keep it in the bottom of your drawer

and remember Aunt Amy, and under it you might slide
the letter you wrote to yourself to be opened on
Christmas when you were an old lady of thirty

to remind you of how it was.

Janet McCann

To Awaken

To wake to the desire for water—
To wake to real human thirst.
This is not boredom or loneliness.

Your hand on the tap,
A twist of the chrome bar,
Clear liquid flows into the glass—

You take a moment to watch
Its shimmers of light
Under the soft lamp,
And then you sip, feel
Coolness running down your hot throat,
The tight body relaxing.

To be grateful without complications.

John Grey

Comet

We were out on the back porch,
staring skyward,
awaiting the return of the comet.
My mother was amazed yet disbelieving
that astronomers could predict such things.

My father talked of the wild-eyed preacher
he had seen downtown
who said this cosmic visitation was
a billboard for God's anger.
With exaggerated gestures
and a voice like a used-car salesman
gone berserk,
he had raged that only my father's
immediate repentance
could steer such intergalactic vengeance
away from earth.
My father said he'd humored the man
by adopting the benign smile of a convert,
before rushing off to the parking garage,
the highway, and our home.
For some reason, though,
he did decide to speak more kindly
of our neighbor George from that day on.

We children could barely bottle our excitement,
though whether it was from what
the sky would tell
or the late night hour,
I could not say.

Finally, we saw
a dazzle of lights like
closely clustered stars.
"Will the world end?"
my little sister asked,
as seriously as she could.
My mother patted her head,
as she did when touch
spoke with greater wisdom than words.
I remember the ensuing silence,
the fresh night air,
hearts on high-wire,
eyes glued to the heavens.

Had someone looked down from the sky,
they would have seen
a household comet,
frozen in space,
scouring the Milky Way
for its sparkling reflection.

Orman Day

My Stolen Canoe

Who paddled my stolen canoe through the debris of Katrina's breaching waters? Did the thief sell my boat to a hero who rescued families from wave-slapped rooftops and ferried the dead from tree limbs to a dryer place? Or did my canoe become a corsair, filled to its gunwales with looted jewels and leather jackets?

In St. Paul, Minnesota, during the summer of 2002, I made real a boyhood dream. I bought that long green canoe and started down the Mississippi.

Paige, a poet friend, taught me to sweep and draw with a paddle, to arc the poles of a dome tent. She was thirty-one and more the pessimist. I was a generation older.

At times, we brought the canoe ashore, so that we could find a café for lunch or coffee. She would caution that we should hide the canoe. I waved away her fears. I said, "We can't take this voyage without believing in benevolence."

We paddled down the river for weeks, drinking sodas handed us by strangers, accepting rides to convenience stores, and sleeping in vacant lots. At night, the view of whole lighted towns was spectacular.

In Saint Francisville, Louisiana, Paige left in a rental car with John. She said she preferred to ride to New Orleans.

I introduced myself to Juliette.

Just south of Baton Rouge, in Saint Gabriel, a city named for a messenger, Juliette and I stowed the canoe on brush and rock and went back to her farmhouse. There, we listened to the news.

Swirling in the Gulf of Mexico, Hurricane Isadore threatened to tangle the river with shingles and trees and drowning cows.

The next morning, Juliette drove us back to the riverbank in her rattling pickup truck. My canoe was gone. I was tempted to curse the thief. I hoped that he capsized in a ring of water moccasins and alligators. My tears ran in rivulets. I shook. Not in anger but in disappointment. I felt sorry for a thief who didn't care whose dreams he dashed.

A few days later, after Isadore had veered and softened, I stepped ashore from Juliette's canoe, at Audubon Park. I smiled in weary triumph and kissed the rain-moist earth. I knew that my canoe possessed a destiny I could not know or control.

In 2005 came those images of Katrina, and I remembered my canoe. I prayed that my loss was no loss, but a gift I had given. I wondered who had paddled my canoe through the debris of Katrina's breaching waters.

Wally Swist

The Locomotive

You ask me if I will remember our passion.
We are seated beside a window in a Pullman,

passing through the countryside in spring.
A signpost of a village flashes before our eyes.

There is a red barn beside the station, a pond
reflecting sky, and pink blossoms falling above

the white chickens. Traveling in the locomotive
of the heart, we must always try to appraise

what we can keep and how much
of the extraordinary we must learn to let go of;

how much of us, as limitless as passion can be,
will remain; how we may be able

to break past that, to find ourselves,
more aware of a radiance than a blinding light,

destined, as we are, to arrive
somewhere between moving and standing still.

Wally Swist

The Tide

Whenever I recall the lifetime
      I was a mariner, I see myself
            at a distance, as I look out

across the sea, returning
      with a cache of pearls in urns
            of delphinium blue, the deck

loaded with oysters in baskets
      of Tyrolean wicker.
            She had seen me off, centuries,

millennia ago, the purple ribbons
        in her hair blowing above her shoulders.
                I carried with me the memory

of the shape of her breasts, the taste
        of her skin burning on my tongue.
                Unable to navigate the unseen

reef in the channel, I was lost
        in a wreck, in a rush of waves, the hull
                splintering against rocks, my body

floating away among the deep-sea rooms,
        veil after veil of schools of passing fish
                fluctuating in trapezoidal walls.

When I recall my lifetime
        as a mariner, I watch her
                from a distance, as she looks out

across the sea, waiting—
        expecting me to be carried by the tide,
                to return to the harbor of her arms.

Julie Mars

Anybody Any Minute

It was much later, after she'd returned home, after she'd finished her watering and weeding, that Ellen realized she had not told Rayfield about Tommy's confessed interest in another woman. So he had not asked her that final question—"What are you gonna do?"—in response to anything that had happened on the surface. Rather, he had intuited that she, like he, was in the midst of a marriage meltdown. How did he know? Was she an open book? Or was Rayfield just unusually adept at reading subtext?

She moved so she could rest her back against the bark of the maple tree at the end of the driveway. Mutley, his head resting on her thigh, gazed deeply into her eyes. She pressed lightly along his browridges and ran her fingers along the length of his nose. Olivier, squatting like a rice paddy worker, played in the grass several yards away.

Suddenly, Ellen felt the air pressure shift, as if her ears needed to pop. The afternoon sun on her neck, the softness of Mutley's fur coat, the rhythm of Olivier's babbling—it seemed so precious.

Ellen had once insisted that a friend drive her out into the middle of the country at midnight and drop her off. She wanted to walk around in the dark and listen to the sounds of nature. Walden Pond seemed an obvious choice, and when Ellen stepped out of her friend's VW van there, she felt like a spiritual anthropologist. She watched the taillights on the van disappear and then tiptoed down to the lake. Every tree was her brother, and every rock, her sister, and she experienced indescribable bliss when she stripped off her clothes and plunged into the water.

This moment, under her own maple tree, had some of that magic.

I have to write a mission statement, she suddenly realized. Now, when I'm in this state. But if she moved, ran into the house for a pen and paper, she would disturb Mutley, who seemed supremely happy.

Ellen didn't like to think unless she had a pen in her hand. Important thoughts got away, like wild animals, unless they were tied down with ink. But today, for the preliminary work on her personal life mission statement, she would have to wing it. She was certain that crafting a mission statement, one that not only reflected her past values but also required her to be, in the future, more than she already was, would put her life back on track. It would clarify her essential essence and allow her to eliminate all unproductive, useless activity. A mission statement was like a lucky charm, a talisman, or a medicine bag.

But when she tried to think forward, a curtain was stretched across her field of vision like the thick velvet drapes of a Broadway stage. In Ellen's youth, even the neighborhood movie theaters had such a curtain—two curtains, actually: A heavy outer one and a translucent inner one. Each separated and pulled away from its other half, the bottom gracefully fluttering like a party dress. Watching the curtains part had symbolic significance. It meant that real life had been beaten back, surrendered to an alternative world.

If her future were a movie, though, Ellen had no idea of the genre. She had bought her ticket blindfolded. She felt the ultraviolet rays of the sun penetrating the layer of skin that was beginning to sag off her cheek and jawbones. The warmth seemed to open her mind, and suddenly she realized that, throughout female stages one and two, the first and second movie features of her life, she had held the image of *ipsissimus*, she who is most herself, in her mind as her goal. Obviously *ipsissimus* had been the nutshell version of her unconscious mission statement. But because she had not formalized it, because it had been more of a philosophical musing than a practical battle plan, she had often strayed. She had forgotten about it for days, months, and years on end. Mission statements, like posters demonstrating the Heimlich maneuver, had to be posted in a prominent place and reread daily as a practical reminder.

"Sorry, Mutley," she said as she extracted herself from underneath him and ran to snatch her stenographer's notebook from the car seat. When she returned to her spot under the tree, Mutley had not even lowered his head, and she was able to slip right back into her previous spot.

She flipped open the notebook, wrote "Mission Statement" across the top of a blank page, held her pen poised at the left margin, and gazed out over the vegetable patch, expecting inspiration. The blank page had never been a problem for Ellen.

Words wanted to form themselves and jump onto paper for her. She could no more avoid them than the Titanic could have avoided the iceberg.

But like the iceberg, much of the self she was headed toward was submerged. She could sense its presence in the waters of her unconscious, but she wasn't exactly sure where it was or what it would look like when she finally crashed into it. Her mission had something to do with love, she knew, though maybe that was only the temporary side effect of Dr. Yi's tea. To do good work fit in somewhere, but Ellen wasn't convinced that that originated inside of her. It could be a legacy of her Catholic upbringing—something that was pounded into her head by nuns in black habits before she ever knew that extreme selfishness was the option of choice for most people who accomplished anything in life.

She looked down at the notebook in her lap. And then, as if it were written there, a memory asserted itself. For Ellen, it was like watching a home video, twenty years old. She was sitting at her kitchen table in her apartment on Thompson Street in the city. The clock she could see in her mind read 1:05. Fifty-five minutes until her psychotherapy appointment. In front of her was a legal pad, and she was in the process of making a list of all the ways she hated herself. She had taken on this bizarre task because, the previous week, amidst her sobs about the state of her life, she had blurted out a sentence she had lived to regret: "I should be looking for a job," she had confessed to her therapist, "but instead, I'm making a list of all the ways I hate myself! It's already five pages long." Carried away with the drama of the moment, she had exaggerated quite a lot. In fact, under the influence of a Thai stick, she had undertaken the chore of listing her worst traits, but had run out of steam after the first five, which were hardly hot news to her: Financial screwup, slothful, directionless, promiscuous, oversensitive.

"Why don't you bring your list in next week?"

"What?" Ellen had asked, busted.

"Your list."

"Okay," she'd said blankly as she watched Marcia, her shrink, trace small circles on her kneecap with her fingers. Ellen, a deep-sea diver exploring the subconscious world of her psyche, had thought of Marcia as her buoy on the surface. Twice a week, she'd seen her. Ellen had relied on it.

Not wanting to be caught in a fib, Ellen had worked hard on her self-hatred list. Her tendency to decorate the simple truth to make it more entertaining was a trait she was trying to discourage. She called her little lies phantom facts, creative amplifications, or permutations on the original. Ellen had a whole vocabulary of euphemisms, but in her heart, she knew they were lies, and she gave herself no credit for her rich imagination. "I'm a liar," she added to her list, bringing it one line closer to the bottom of page one. I waste time. I am resentful of people who have it easy. I do not live up to my full potential. I bear grudges. I drink too much. I am petty.

On and on she went, flinging every insult she could think of into her own face. She even tried to recall the Ten Commandments so she could document the ones she routinely broke. Because it was essentially a mental exercise, she didn't cry. But when she reached the middle of page three, she threw her pen across the tiny apartment and abandoned the task.

A half hour later, she had told Marcia the truth. "So there I am, sitting at my kitchen table, trying to come up with five pages of things I hate about myself. There are thirty-five lines per page, you know, so that's a hundred and seventy-five separate things. I got to a hundred and I said, 'Forget it.' "

"Congratulations," said Marcia. "Did you bring the list?"

"No, I threw it in the garbage." Another phantom fact. It was laying in wait on the table, exactly where she'd left it when she had fled to her appointment. Ellen went directly from therapy to her waitressing job and didn't arrive home until midnight. She was slightly tipsy, as usual, and had forgotten all about the legal pad and list. She swept it onto the floor, the Jack Daniel's she'd consumed in a bar on the corner temporarily bringing out the swashbuckler in her.

But something made her pick it up again. She turned out the lights and lit a candle. She placed her boom box on the table, and put on her most beautiful nightgown, ice green with spaghetti straps that crossed in the back, worn only on the most special of occasions. She pressed the record button and read her list. At the end, she burned the three pages to ashes, leaving the recorder going until the last crackle of the fire had ceased and only the honking of horns on the street below could be heard in her apartment. She labeled the tape "Adios, self-hatred" and hid it among her most private papers. She had never listened to it again.

The memory made her sad. There was no way to measure suffering, and compared to the starving people in Africa and the children from war-torn countries in Eastern Europe who had seen their parents blown apart before their eyes, hers had been minimal. But at that moment, her heart ached for her younger self, for all the pain she had had to bear. The intensity of her suffering, necessary or not, had brought Ellen to her knees to beg for mercy many times in her twenties.

When she was younger, she tended to define herself by the "nots." I am not disciplined, not confident, not rich, and so on. In its inimitable way, even her unconscious cooperated, offering her nightly dreams of knots in her hair (and Ellen, without a comb) or knots in her stomach (and Ellen, with no supply of Valium). Somehow the creation of the list she now remembered, her list of flaws that she later burned to ashes, had initiated the "not phase." It was as if her refusal to scorn herself, as symbolized by the burning, had gone haywire, and suddenly, she'd become the negative of her former self.

Now, she suddenly realized, she was transitioning back to a positive image, like a photographic print submerged in the waters of a chemical bath. She was thinking in terms of "I am" instead of "I am not." Her notebook was in her lap, a patch of white in a sea of green grass. Without thinking, she wrote, "To do good and be love."

Her writing hand fell to her side, and she stared in shock at what she had written. The simplicity of the mission statement left no room for misinterpretation, but where had it come from? She had expected something more of herself, perhaps along the lines of "To see my documentary on Rodney at the Cannes Film Festival" or "To remove the slugs from under the rocks of my personal psyche."
Quickly, she closed her notebook.

In the sixties, she'd proudly worn a "Make Love, Not War" button on her fringed leather vest. Perhaps, all things considered, she hadn't changed that much, though there was a certain aggressive resistance to the "make love" statement that had evaporated from the words she had written inside her closed book.

She opened it again and found the right page. Could that really be her mission statement as she approached the portal of the crone phase? Be and do, do and be, she thought: The two big verbs of everybody's native tongue. Essence and action. She could certainly handle the "do good" half of her mission statement. She simply had to choose the righteous path in each moment. Each action had to be held up against an image of unselfish goodness. She looked down at Mutley. She had saved him from life in the dog pound. That was good. And she had taken Olivier without a split second's hesitation. That was the right and good thing to do in that moment. She was growing organic vegetables, tending to Mother Earth, pulling weeds with her bare hands and lugging water back and forth across the lawn with the cheerfulness of a Zen monk. She was helping Rayfield cope, saying short prayers on behalf of Cocho, and preparing to bring the down-home sweetness of Rodney de Beer to a wider audience. In a way, she felt that she was even doing good on behalf of Viola. She was getting people to talk about her, draining the swamp of unsaid words that festered and stunk. At the present moment, she was a veritable ambassador of goodness, even by her own objective standards.

But being love? That was a different ball game. What did it mean? Ellen didn't even know how to think about it. Maybe it was like being a radio transmitter. You just pulsated in private, there for anyone who wanted to tune in. But what did you transmit? What was love anyway?

An old boyfriend, rarely brought to mind for a guest appearance, had defined it as being totally hungry and totally satisfied at the same time. But that was genus love, species sexual. That was lust and passion, which figured prominently in making love but had nothing to do with being love. Loving Olivier, loving Mutley, loving Rodney—in all these examples, Ellen thought, the love had pressed on her from the inside out, giving her a physical sensation she couldn't ignore. It was too powerful to contain, so saying the words "I love you" was like begging for mercy. But being love, that was different. It relied on neither a recipient nor a possible payoff. It was a paradox: To remain in that state would require total concentration, but maintaining the focus was something that you did. And be was not do. Maybe if you did long enough, though, it was possible to just be.

Excerpted from Julie Mars' novel Anybody Any Minute (St. Martin's Press, 2008)

W. K. Lawrence

The Fish

Okay, so she got me,
My mouth around her
Hidden silver hook.
She didn't fight.
She didn't need to.
She reeled me in pound by pound,
Blinded and vulnerable,
My fins still,
Knowing
There was no longer
Water to swim.
The air sucked at me.
I peered 'round.

She stood above,
Our hearts beating,
Her hair blowing,
Her gentle fingers holding
My coarse white flesh,

Holding me.
Her mouth tightened,
And I felt
A sharp pinch
As she slipped the hook
Out and
Laid me down.

I gasped for water.
My body began to shake,
Not because of
The silver blade,
Reflecting light,
Somebody handed her,
But because life has a way
Of fighting for you
In those last moments.

I looked into her eyes,
Full
Of life.
The browns, the greens, and
The yellows of coral

Mixed with
Sky and ocean blues.

She stroked my skin,
And with a smile,
With the blow of a kiss,
She let me slide
From her fingers
Back into the sea,
And then,
She jumped in too.

John Fitzpatrick

Habits

In the afternoon of this fourth day
of fast and cleansing, I desire
so much those croissants,
biscotti, and latté bought
daily at the local patisserie. There

        in Paris you sit sipping
your café au lait, planning your day.
        A waiter brings you the croissant
I want so very much. Later the arms
of a lover will hold you in his greeting.

Here is where I want
to revise happenings, as if to rewrite what
I so gallantly wrote—*I was following
another path*—and denying what I really
wanted all along.

Carol Emshwiller

The Meaning of the Fields

All this beauty, and you want meaning, too? All these sunsets. All the animals that slither by, creep and crawl. You want a worm that turns *and* turns into a butterfly? You want such a worm to be a sign of something beyond itself? As if I would turn into something that means something. As if I would shed my skin and shine out golden or silvery. As if my eyes would turn blue?

You, on the other hand, are, I suppose, how one ought to be. Marching, stomach first, onto the battlefield of life, or, more likely, any field that happens to be by the roadside across from the ditch. You don't stumble. You plan ahead. You foresee what needs to be foreseen.

I suppose you think that even I would have a reason for being, were my nose exactly what a nose should be. You think that then my life would have a meaning way above washing dishes.

See how you point your chin at the sun to estimate the zenith and all the other high points right from your own front door. You turn then and measure "the angle of repose" of the scree that drops away from my front porch.

You nod, but not at me.

You have said there's even meaning in trees. You have said, and more than once, that nobody can say there isn't.

I say a tree is just a tree and all the better for it.

We are not a beautiful people. None of us. Not even you. We have eyes with droopy lids. We have bumps on our noses. Our hair is lank. We hunch and hump along. It gets us there.

I go up and sit on my rock and look out at the fields below. I presume that if there had been a rainbow across the valley, as there so often is, you'd think, as you so often do, that it was yet another sign for you to ask me to marry you.

As I come back down, past your house, I trip on one of your vines. I fall flat and bump my chin, which wasn't the greatest chin in the first place.

Gets me to thinking, as you always do, that meanings abound and in the oddest places. Here's a whole new meaning. That's because I see you seeing me fall, but you don't come to help me up.

I suppose, if I wanted better—a better place to live and a different you—I'd walk away into the woods, a little bit farther than my usual walk, build myself a lean-to and live on berries. I'd make pets of everything that happened by. I'd tell each one, "You're nothing but yourself, just as I am me." I'd say, "There are no similes," as if anything were ever like anything else, and they'd all take joy in that.

I sit a little while, right in front of your house, and catch my breath. I knew you wouldn't come and help. You probably put out those vines just to trip me up.

Out loud I say, "What if meanings turn back on themselves and become the opposite of each other, twist and roll? What then?"

It's not the first time I've said that.

You pretend not to hear.

I check my ankle. It hurts, and it's starting to swell up.

I say, "What if a rainbow, upside down, becomes a ship of many colors?"

But it doesn't matter what I say. You've already gone inside.

"You misjudge me if you think I'm helpless," I say. I limp away.

I ought to cater to you, as Mother said I should, before she died. She wanted us to marry, but I'm trying to find others of our people. Surely, there are some of us left, somewhere. They would be lank-haired, like me, and pale-eyed. They would have lumpy noses.

Mother kept saying our talent would die out if we didn't marry our own kind, and who else is there around here but you?

But I always said, "What talent? For shooting jackrabbits? For kicking the cat?"

"You'd be surprised," she said.

I know all about our so-called talent—just one. It's the ability to slide. A *glissando* to the side when suddenly attacked. Not much there that's odd or magical. I can't think when I've ever needed it. I imagine it was life-saving back in more primitive times, when we were faced with tigers.

Well, if you put out vines to trip me, and then don't come to help me up, I figure you've about given up on me—ever agreeing to marry you, that is.

Mother always said, "All right, then. Go on. Find some others of us if you must. Take your pug nose right on out the door." And I always did, but only for an afternoon. Maybe it's time to really head off, sprained ankle, bloody chin, and all. I'll wrap my leg up tight, and I'll take Mother's cane.

I wash the dishes, sweep the house, make myself a sandwich, grab an apple, and go.

When I was a teenager and looking, even way back then, for a suitable lover, I never went this far into the mountains. Now, on purpose, I keep going until I've gone too far to come back tonight. I may be sorry. The weather doesn't look that great. I wrap up in my rain poncho and rest under a gnarled old juniper.

I say, "Look how beautiful this old tree is, and look how it means nothing but itself."

I'm still talking to you, even way out here.

Now who of my kind, or of any kind in their right mind, would be out here this time of year? Am I looking for love from a mule deer?

A storm comes. Hail and lightning. I leave my tree and hurry down the slope to find a sheltered spot. I run hard on my sprained ankle. I'll bet I won't be able to walk at all tomorrow.

I find a good spot. A sort of indentation, just my size, in the edge of a cliff. It keeps me dry, if I curl up and keep my toes tucked in. I watch the lightning from here. You'd say it's just like the Fourth of July, but I say it's just lightning in the forest.

Before the storm stops, I fall asleep.

In the morning, I uncurl. It's a wonderful, bright day. I stand up and yell without meaning to. Not because of the pain in my ankle, but because of the view and the day. I'm in a gorgeous valley I never saw before. Full of lupine and fireweed and shooting star. I thought I had run towards home when the hail started, but I don't think so. I have no idea where I am. I couldn't go home if I wanted to.

You'd have said my yell was because of the meanings of this glade, but my yell was because this glade is a really nice one. It's so beautiful. I even think I'll yell again.

Now I've scared a doe and her fawn. I didn't notice them 'til they ran. Goodness knows what else I scared. There's the flap of wings. If there are people nearby, then surely they heard me, too.

I hobble over and sit behind some scraggly bushes. They won't hide me, but better them than nothing. I keep quiet and wait to see what else I've stirred up.

You'd think my kind would be living out here in this hanging meadow. It's a perfect place. Especially for short ugly folk who don't own much of anything.

I see a patch of Solomon's Seal. I see miner's lettuce, elderberries, mountain currants. Lots to eat, if one knows how to look.

I wait. I hold still.

And somebody does come. He must have heard me, but now he looks as if he forgot about it. Maybe I sounded more like a bird than a person. My yell was a kind of squawk.

He's not at all my kind, but as to ugliness, he might as well be. He has a long, boney face, instead of a round puffy one like ours. He has fuzzy black eyebrows, instead of those that hardly show at all. I'm quite taken with him.

But it's not berries he's picking. It's flowers. I wonder for whom. I catch my breath with yearning.

I always did like black hair and hooked noses, and that lanky, loose look. Just the opposite of me. He's probably as farsighted as I am nearsighted. If I should marry him, and if our children were half him and half me, they would turn out just exactly right.

Then, for heaven's sake, he sits down almost right in front of me, hums a tuneless song, and takes out his lunch. Watercress…can that be? Watercress sandwiches?

I've eaten all my food long ago. I'm hungry, and I love watercress. Now, I catch my breath with a different kind of yearning.

I wonder if I should…

I do. I come out from behind my bush. I smile.

I'm sure I look eager. Much too much so. He leans away from me and holds his sandwich close to his chest. He's definitely not happy to see me. Or is it just that I startled him? Perhaps opposites don't always attract.

"I was wondering if you could spare a tiny bite or two. I haven't eaten since yesterday."

He squints at me with disapproval, exactly as you would do. I recognize that doubting look. Can he be as contrary as you are?

"You see, I've sprained my ankle." I limp back and forth to show how hurt I am. I exaggerate, but only a little.

He breaks off a small piece. I sit down beside him, as close as I dare. I say, "I need to rest, because of my ankle."

There's the sound of the stream and the rustle of leaves. Why don't I stop talking and listen and eat?

"Even now, with my sore ankle, I can fry up little birds."

He looks interested.

"I presume that you have many children who look just like you, and a wife for whom you gather flowers."

"I have no children and no wife."

"Perfect!"

I say it out loud, though I didn't mean to.

How deep his voice is, unlike yours, and growly as a—but none of that. Suffice it to say, deep and growly.

I can fall in love at first sight as well as the next person, but I'd better back off a bit so as not to scare him. Actually, it's a wonder he doesn't object to my following him home.

Once you said, "Wherever you go, look for the more meaningful places." And here is one, or so you'd say. A village of similes, where everything is exactly like everything else, even more than like itself. The huts stand as if out of storybooks. The trees are gnarled, as if from the top of a windy mountain. There's a Main Street, looking as if it went somewhere beyond this valley, though I don't think it does, and now there's me, the short dumpy stranger, limping into town. A pilgrim in search of, I don't know what, except in search of this very man right here.

My, what nice tall people everybody is. I could love them all. Some would say I'm the exact right kind of person to marry one of them.

We pass three women. You would say three is a significant number, but I like four better. Am I being contrary for contrary's sake?

"If you could see your way clear to sparing a little gingerbread or apple pie?" I say to one of them. (It's a gingerbread kind of a place, though here I am thinking just the way you always do and asking what you'd ask. If they don't have any, it's your kind of a mistake I've made.) "Or do you live on elderberries and Solomon's Seal?"

They're wearing high heels that make them look even taller and slimmer, and make me look even shorter and dumpier. But why heels? Maybe just around the corner and over the hill there is a city. Maybe Main Street does actually go somewhere.

"How many long miles, or, on the other hand, short miles, as the case may be, until I get to a town?"

Even the women have bushy eyebrows and thin lips. What this whole place needs is exactly me. How come this man doesn't see that?

But then, I think he does see. Suddenly, he gives me a look and leads me to his little storybook house.

It's a mess in there. For sure, he doesn't have a woman to look after him.

Not a word is spoken, nor need there be. All the better, considering what words do. In spite of my sore ankle, I set about cleaning up and cooking what's at hand. There's a pail of crayfish.

Isn't it odd that, in all these years of living next door, I've never cooked for you?

So, the man of my dreams and I sit in his tiny yard and eat what I've made. It's delicious, but he doesn't say so any more than you would.

We watch the sunset, also without saying anything. Just before the sun pops below the mountain behind us, and the sky is full of wispy red clouds, I do say, "I like children."

He gives me a look. You would say a disconcerted look. I'd just say a long look. What could be more romantic than his piercing black eyes?

About the sleeping arrangements, the cottage has only one room. I can see that the man of my dreams isn't ready to welcome me into his bed. I'm not quite ready for that either. After all, I hardly know him. And when a person doesn't talk much…

You're the one I know. I can always tell exactly what you're going to say next. Like right now, you'd say I should get out of here before it's too late. Well, I'm not going to.

He doesn't say, "Take the bed." He says, "Take the floor." And so I do.

How wonderfully long and flat he looks in bed.

Next morning, I'm right there, first thing, with the tea and toast and elderberry jam. You wouldn't have thought I would be this way at all, but I am.

And look how I'm agreeing and agreeable. I say, "You've found the perfect place to live in harmony with your own kind. I understand that and respect it. But don't you think there's need for new…um…blood? For the sake of the children?"

He doesn't think so.

"One's own kind is so ordinary."

"If you say so."

When would you have said any such thing?

"I do say so," I say.

He's thinking about it. At least that.

"You need a change."

He's not the sort to argue. He shrugs. He doesn't care either way. What a nice change from you.

But he likes his own kind best. It's what I like, too. His kind, I mean. Look how he sits with his boney knees pointing, one towards the door and the other towards the window.

I say, "My love," as I look off towards one of his trees. I suppose he thinks I love the tree—which I do, but in a whole different way.

And then, we have our fight, where my special talent, my *glissando*, almost saves me, and his special talent, an opposite kind of *glissando*, makes it possible for him to slap me anyway.

Just before our fight, he had me do things on purpose to make me not want to be there. He had me wash the sheets. He had me change the bed but not lie in it. I suppose he thought my love for him would be my reward. Do I look like a servant? I suppose to his tall, lanky kind, I do.

I'd said, "I'm leaving." And right after that, I had my slap.

Now, I hobble away. I've stolen his basket, so that along the way I can pick berries. I go farther and farther, all the way up a hill, then down into the next valley.

And then I find you. Or, rather, you find me.

"What are you doing way out here," I say. "Looking for somebody to torment? Or did you discover that you couldn't live without me?"

You say, and right away, "I give up on the meaning of the fields."

"Now you say it."

You've never looked uglier. Hair, what there is left of it, sticking out in all directions, like a fence around the prairie of your bald head. I think I feel something like tenderness.

I say, "All our children will be just like us. I hope you know that."

I hand you the berries and say, "For you," just as if they really were.

"It'll be as if…" you say, or start to, but you stop right in the middle.

On the way back, you help me over the rough spots, because of my ankle. On the smooth spots, you hold my hand. We hike down to our little houses, where—except for arguments and similes and meanings and occasionally tripping each other up on our paths to and fro—and where, to me, nothing is ever like anything else except itself, though to you everything is like something else, though we say so less now—we live happily ever after.

Maggie Jochild

Summer at Sweetwell

She's picking it up: Not just the bags
of organic chick starter and pig corn
she's to grind for slop, using the mill
belted to the old Farmall tractor,

Or how to skid behemoths of Doug fir
and Western Red Cedar with a team
of sister Belgian drafthorses, who
follow into ferny bottoms, stand in
earned trust and then haw, with bunched
muscle, all the way uphill, logs
to be skinned and bladed into cants.
She's learning stack art, the ziggurats
of musty hay sandwiched with chicken dung,
ready for tomorrow's spread onto market fields
lying fallow this rotation. She's skimming cream
from shiny cans of warm milk and coming
home from an afternoon at the U-pick
with eighteen pounds of blueberries.

She's finding how to live with both
hands full, not born into it—a turn
she made to take in hand the links
leading back to unlit family memory.
Ten thousand years of uneasy dominion.
Meals to be worked off. Harvest
she shares to believe she deserves.

Brett Gadbois

Perfect

Lately, Josie's been putting the screws to me. Sometimes it's a subtle little I'm-gonna-slide-this-information-into-the-conversation-and-see-if-he-blinks kind of thing. Other times it's an out and out, "Hey, listen up, Buster. I'm talkin' here," kind of deal. It's about love—that's what it is. Who ever gets enough of it? I know I don't. I didn't in my marriage, and from everything she's told me, I'm sure Josie didn't either.

Josie calls it her cavern of unmet needs. This is good for me to visualize 'cause I see myself on the lip of a cliff, high atop a backhoe, grinding the gears, teetering on the edge, working and sweating, half-covered in dust, trying to fill the damn thing up.

I can't. Of course, no one on earth can. This is a point of friction with us. A bone of contention.

Her kids had gone to California with her ex, and my ex had taken our boy camping, so Josie and I got to spend some "unsupervised" time together last week.

I don't know what it is about sex. It seems to be both perfect union and the doorway to a million misunderstandings. We've been having electrifying, soulful, connected sex. We've been having angular eruptions and emotional fractures and fissures as well. The kind of stuff where one of us will say something, and the other will feel pounced on and mistreated. Then, the one who said the trip-wire thing will pout, withdraw, and start to worry about saying anything at all.

Sometimes, I feel like one of those guys in the army, feeling his way over dangerous pastures and broken roads with a mine detector.

We made love on a Sunday afternoon, after one of our close call boy-we-nearly-stepped-on-it-this-time episodes. It was satisfying and resonant. Afterwards, we ate a leisurely dinner. We went to bed and made love again.

When I woke in the morning, Josie was nowhere in sight. I found her on the couch in the living room. I figured I'd kept her up by snoring or thrashing around in bed. I started the coffee brewing.

"So," I said, "why'd you bail out on me last night?"

She leaned up against the kitchen counter and frowned. "Sometimes, I need to distance myself. It's 'cause I get too needy," she said. "I start to want all these things, and I know I'm not going to get 'em."

"Like what?" I ask, thinking about the backhoe.

"Like you telling me you love me."

"Oh," I said, handing her a mug of coffee. "That."

The truth is, I am a little skittish about the whole I-love-you business. I behave in loving ways with Josie, but I don't say the words. I don't have any trouble telling my son that I love him. I lean over to tell him when he's drawing a picture of a volcano.

I smooth his unkempt curls, smell and kiss his tender head. My son doesn't have to reciprocate. He doesn't have to lift a finger. He doesn't even have to look at me. I'm reassured. I'm standing on a rock in an ocean of love. My faith is unshakable.

I've talked about this a number of times with Josie. We agree on this: She needs to hear it, but I need to be able to say it or not say it. I guess I've brought the shattered pieces of my former marriage to this relationship.

Jen and I were married for twelve years. I did my darndest to fill her to the brim with unconditional love. I was determined to make it work. Somehow my efforts were always half a cup for her. If only I'd tried harder, jumped higher, or stepped up to the plate, she'd say. I think Superman or Buddha would've had their work cut out for them.

It doesn't do me a bit of good to rag her down though. What's done is done. We're done, and I'm not sorry. I reached a saturation point with the marriage. Like a towel that falls into the water. At some point it can't get any more soaked. That's how I got—soaked to the bone. When I knew that my best just wasn't good enough, I was free. Like a hollow reed rattling in the bitter wind. Like cattails at the edge of a frozen lake. All raw, achy, and lonesome. Lonesome, alone, and free.

This explains why I'm taking it slow with Josie. I no longer have any desire to turn myself into Zamora, the triple-jointed wonder, or Lon Chaney, the man with a thousand faces. If this one doesn't please you, darlin', how about this one? How about a beard, a moustache, dark glasses, a shaved head? What if I stand on my head and sing the Star Spangled Banner?

Josie called on Tuesday night. I'd just finished my dinner, a salad pulled fresh from the garden. It was one of those rare summer evenings when the temperature is just right, with a little breeze to lift the air out of the doldrums. The sun rippled through the trees at the edge of the pasture across from my place. I took the phone out onto the deck, and we talked.

She told me about her day. Work politics. Controlling managers, manipulators, and overworked peons. This last was the group she belonged to. I listened for a while. Then, we talked about our weekend. We talked about her sleeping on the couch.

She started nudging me again about the I-love-you stuff. My neck and shoulders tensed up. I tried to re-explain my position on our conundrum, but there's something relentless in Josie, when she gets this way. I felt like I was slipping on smooth rocks in a rushing creek. My voice rose, but she kept after me.

Finally, I said, "Ok, ok. I can't fill in all the blanks for you. I can't make whatever didn't work out in your marriage all cozy and comfortable right here and now. But I want you to listen for a few minutes. That's all. Then you can talk 'til your heart's content, and I'll listen back."

She was silent.

"I want you to try to imagine that this is perfect. And that you and I are immersed and dissolved in perfection." I surveyed my unkempt, weed-choked yard strewn with my boy's Supersoaker water gun, empty plastic flowerpots, and a high-priced worthless trike he'd outgrown and hardly ever used.

"This is it. This is perfect—us on the phone, the sun going down, and your teenage daughter angry with you 'cause you're going out with me. It's perfect with Sam's toys all over the living room, the stains I can't seem to get rid of, and that persistent odor, left over from the previous owner's lax attitude about kitty hygiene, that hangs over my couch like a ghost. This is it—the top of Mount Everest," I said. I studied the weathered top of my deck that could use another coat of oil. "We're lucky if we get to see each other once a week. Darn right, we're lucky. I'm standing, and you're breathing. How lucky can you get? We've got our sorrows and our tears, you and I. We both have kids with somebody else, but we're surviving. We're working long hours, and we're muddling through. We're supervised by inconsiderate bosses who are stressed about the bottom line. We're paying too much for small, sagging houses. My lawn needs a mow, and the blackberry bushes are threatening to take over my apple tree. I'm tired, and so are you. And you know what else?"

"What?" she said.

"We've been in love for a long time. You and me and the red-tipped lettuce leaves. The crows cawing and nesting nearby. That tall pine, with the hammock swaying peacefully beneath it, in your back yard. Dandelions standing in my rock garden. Your girl falling asleep in your arms and my boy waking up and clutching a quarter the tooth fairy left him in the night. We've melted in hot showers, you and I. I've been lost in space, when I've held your hand. I've taken a walk through the stars, when I've kissed your neck and smelled the faint scent of your lavender soap and sweat. I've been transported who-knows-where by your kisses and been to the moon and back from just one of your sidelong, happy glances. I've been extinguished, how many times, when we've made love? Who can count them? Who would want to? And I've come back to my body dazed, wondering where I've been. Back to being a separate guy in a chaotic world. Back to business as usual."

She was silent.

"Back to being a man on the phone who will go to bed alone tonight. Might even think of his sweetheart falling asleep next to her skinny, boney daughter."

I heard her exhale.

"You're right," she said. "I slept on the couch so I wouldn't have to do this."

"You don't have to do it. You can disengage any time you want to. So can I. That's the price we pay for love. The high cost of living. It's scary as hell to stand up in the blast furnace without a stitch on. I'm scared too."

"If you're not scared, you're a saint, or crazy, or just plain out of it," she said.

"Just let it be what it is."

"That's good," she said. "I'm gonna write that down. Put it on my refrigerator until I have it memorized. Maybe even make a t-shirt out of it."

"Listen," I said. "I've gotta go. I think my ear's gonna fall off, or else I'm gonna have to see about getting a phone surgically attached to it. Are you feeling any better?"

"Yeah," she said. "I hear you. I needed to hear you."

"I guess I have to say this stuff until I'm blue in the face. 'Night, love."

"Good night."

I sit down on the grass in front of the deck. I study the wide swath of blackberries marching across the edge of my property. I lie back and feel the dry grass stubble poke my back and shoulders. The contours are uneven beneath me. I set the phone down and look at the sky. The sun is almost gone now. The tops of the trees are silhouetted. I see a handful of stars and a cirrus cloud above a tree. The cloud's shaped like a half-moon. It looks as if the tree branches are supporting it.

I'm supported like that cloud. The night is before me, and the whole world lies at my back. The grass is growing quietly, steadily behind my ears.

P. Kobylarz

What We Do Beyond

It was too cold to bury anything—the second week of February, and the ground was frozen solid. Still, it was funny how the little street was in the process of breaking itself apart. It bee-lined across the ugly part of town and was used to skirt the main road's traffic. Riddled with more than just potholes, whole sections of it were coming unbuckled and sinking, sometimes up to half a foot.

Hardly any cars dared to risk the road. It would save only a few minutes of time to the next stoplight, which would invariably be red. Leaves of last autumn clogged its gutters. The leaves, like the road, were a dirty brown in color. The abandoned house on the hill that overlooked the street was marked with a billboard that clearly stated, "Keep Out."

There on our lawn, under the bare branches of the elm tree, it lay. A dead squirrel. It still looked alive. Its coat of fur and the bushy hair of its tail moved in the wind. The ground beneath it was hard and solid.

We were all aware of the squirrel. Snowdrifts had melted into dirty lumps of powder during a freak revival of spring. Still, Winter had left its calling card in the plowed piles of white-pack. The cold was here to keep the windows secured for months. It had painted them in an opaque crystalline mist. These were only excuses for not noticing.

Our bay window had evaded the gusts of wind. It remained as clear and cold as a slab of ice. Icicles hung from the eaves above it like an ornamental fence spun from glass. Julie had an ability to tell the temperature by placing her hands on the window and blowing on it, making an oval of fog. She was the first to acknowledge the tragedy.

"So what are we going to do about it? The dead thing," she asked.

"What? Who died?" Taylor said.

"You guys know. The squirrel." She pointed past the abstraction of the lamp's glare on the windowpane.

Taylor said he didn't know what she was talking about.

I couldn't figure her melodramatics. It was only road kill. The three of us drove or biked by so many of them everyday. This small town, though still not exactly a city, wasn't all that small anymore. It had sprung up in the flood plain between two forested ridges. Now, the animals of the surrounding woods had a hard time knowing where nature ended and civilization began. Ours was one of those dubiously titled

"Tree Cities." When viewed from a dual-engine shuttle to Minneapolis, the large buildings looked like outcroppings of stone invading a pasture.

"Well, I guess he is sort of our collective pet, but can't we call the dog pound to come out and remove him?"

Julie read the logic of my argument. Still, she wanted immediate action. She couldn't overlook the tragedy as easily as Taylor obviously did, she being the more introspective of the two. They had been married for a year and eight months. The yin-yang aspect of their coupling was emphasized at the moment.

"Couldn't we take care of it?"

"Yeah, sure," Taylor replied from the kitchen, "but not right now. I'm trying to make dinner."

"You mean put it in a plastic bag and leave it on the corner for the garbage men?"

"No, how gross. I don't know what exactly. Something better than that."

Julie stood in her light blue robe and moved the thermostat down a couple of notches. "I'm off to work."

She spun around and ran up the staircase. It took her only minutes to get dressed and leave. Although the weather called for leather boots, warm socks, and thick panty hose, she still painted her toenails red.

After eating the stew of vegetables that Taylor had made for dinner, we thought of ways to occupy our Saturday night. The house was warm with the smells of cooking, and most of the lamps were lit. It was a compact place, with three rooms upstairs and two below, though there was also a garage. Pretty nice for the rent we shared.

I'd recently completed my schooling. I was trying to find work in any major metropolis that would have me. I had had enough of the boondocks. The marginal cities of the northern states offered a distinct lack of opportunity. When my lease had run out, my only two friends in the world had come through and let me move in, "for the time being."

"The time being" implies uncertainty. I tried to do as much as I could. Things like washing the dishes or working on their car. Anything to help them get by. I figured that if my hundred-fold applications for jobs didn't result in anything, I would simply move to the city of my choice. The northwest looked good, at least on maps. Then, there was always California.

Julie worked as a secretary in the hospital. Taylor worked shifts at a data processing company. They'd met at a party after a jazz concert. They'd fallen in love under the rainy skies of summer two years ago. Now, though neither would admit it, the weird hours were putting a strain on their newlywed status. And now, there was this to do.

Taylor was relaxing with a cigarette. His feet were propped on the couch.

"Shall I take care of the matter at hand, or do you want to help me with the honors?" I asked him.

"Give me a few minutes, and we'll both go out." He put his cigarette down to dust off an album, which he then placed gently on the turntable.

The sounds of saxophone and bass were driving from the speakers, as I laced up my boots. The music was not a dirge or one of Albinoni's Adagios, but the mood of the night was struck. Taylor donned his long rancher's coat. We went out into the cold air and streetlights of evening. With the wind chill, the temperature was below zero.

The squirrel's body had acquired a ruffled collar of frost. Its small front paws were held out, clutching nothing.

"The ground's too hard," I said.

Taylor stubbornly trudged to the garage and brought back a shovel. A car drove down the road. Its headlights illuminated his glasses in two quick flashes. He placed the tip of the blade next to the animal and jumped onto the shovel's flat edge. It barely broke into the ground.

"I guess you're right," he said, "but I had to test it. Man, it's cold!"

"Even though I told Julie I wouldn't, why don't I get a garbage bag, you shovel it in, and we go toss it somewhere?"

Taylor acknowledged my suggestion with a nod. He hurled the shovel at the earth one last time, as if it were a javelin.

"Okay, okay. Hurry, I'm freezing."

When I came back, he was balancing the stiff body on the shovel's blade. I held open the mouth of the bag, and he placed the squirrel in with some trepidation.

Then he quipped, "Stick it in the car, and we'll find somewhere to dispose of it. The thing's heavy as a brick." The keys jingled in his pocket. He made for the car. I got in at the passenger's side and dropped the bag onto the floor behind me.

"If this happens again during the summer, Julie will have to deal with the rotting meat," Taylor said. He hit the ignition.

We headed out into the darkness. Neither of us was sure where to go. Taylor said that we wouldn't have to drive far to toss it into the dumpster. A garbage bin behind the supermarket would do the trick. Then, we could let someone else deal with it. The city was responsible for the death anyway.

As we continued driving, I saw a turn-off leading south of town. I had never taken this road. Thirty feet before we approached it, I yelled, "Turn here!"

"Okay, but where the heck are you taking us? This leads to that ghost town of a place, Creek Junction. Beyond that, there's a quarry, and then, nothing."

"Then it's to the quarry."

Not much of the landscape could be seen. It was a night without a moon. I thought I had glimpsed the constellation Leo, but the road turned so many times that I could only keep its tail in view. The hills were dotted with pine and hardwood trees that had grown wild. Although it was winter, the dried grasses stood at chest level. Sometimes the lights of a farmhouse appeared on one of the hills, and we would see the silhouettes of the window frames. They looked like crosses lit from behind. There was nothing else.

About fifteen miles down the road, we saw a sign for the quarry. We pulled up to its dirt road to find a fence that was securely chained with shining new master locks.

"There goes that," Taylor said. "I'm not getting arrested for trespassing."

"Yeah, so let's drive a little farther. We're in the country now. There might be a roadside park or something up ahead."

"There is something up ahead. It's called the Deep South."

"I mean just for a few miles. I've never been this way."

So we continued. Taking corners at forty miles an hour made the bag slide around in the back. We both winced at the sound.

When we came around a bend, we saw the sign for Coon's Marsh. This looked like the place. A red arrow pointed down a gravel stretch that led down a hill. With the brights on, we could tell that the road soon swerved.

Taylor took the sudden turn without slackening his speed. The car left a rooster tail of white dust behind it. This road to nowhere was filled with sinkholes. The ride was getting bumpy, as if we were on a graded mountain road.

The headlights reflected off a shiny surface that was just yards in the distance. When Taylor slowed down for a major rut, I saw pieces of ice floating on it. This was the river. Taylor continued slowly. Then, he stopped altogether and said, "Check that out—"

He positioned the car so that the headlights shone along a length of barbed wire fence that was fastened to rotting poles of wood. Tall yellow grass grew through the fence. We could make out white monoliths of stone in the distance. Barely visible, a string of wire had been manipulated into the word "Beauchamp" within the matrix of the fence. Beyond was a long forgotten cemetery.

"Perfect. Just perfect," he said.

We got out of the car. Taylor found a flashlight in the glove box. I picked up the garbage bag by its neck and held it at arm's length. We hopped the fence. Taylor, way ahead of me, was inspecting the tombstones which stood nearly two feet high.

"This one's from 1879. There's a relief of a dove on it. Pretty weird."

I stood by his side and looked at the ancient marker. The stone next to it was carved with a hand that pointed up. A last hopeful gesture. The few trees left on the outskirts of the plain were creaking in the wind. There were no flowers on the graves. It looked as though no one had been here for years.

"My guess is people from the city have some relatives out here," I said.

"Might be so, but this place is probably closed. Hey, how about that? A cemetery without a waiting list."

"Let's get rid of this thing, before I catch some kind of disease from it."

The land sloped into a field of driftwood, then riverbank. It was Taylor's idea to give the squirrel a burial at sea. We walked down toward the water. We followed the flashlight's yellow beam. Soon, its batteries would be drained, and there could be racoons out this late.

At the river, I turned the bag from its bottom. The squirrel rolled out into the water with a loud plunk. Taylor hummed "Taps" under his breath. Branches, like gnarled arrows breaking the surface of the water, pointed downstream.

As we walked back through the cemetery, we examined the gravestones more carefully. Some were decorated with writing that was too eroded to read. A few of the stones had toppled over, due to the swell of the land. A couple of them were broken in two. The surrounding earth and vegetation looked eager to swallow them up. The rain was staining the stones black. Ashes to ashes, dust to dust? More like bone to ground, bone to ground.

That night in bed, I heard Julie come home. I was having trouble falling asleep, so I'd been studying the patterns that the streetlights made on my ceiling. I was listening to a talk radio station turned down low.

Their bedroom was down the hall from mine, but the hardwood floors and walls transmitted sounds every so often. The wind had to be blowing right. I heard Julie and Taylor talking. They were trying to keep it down, but it sounded like an argument. Then, I heard the click of the light turning off and the bed springs sounding like hungry birds. I covered my head with the blanket. I tried hard to sleep.

The next morning. Julie woke me up by playing the stereo too loudly. It was Sunday. What could I say? I was a guest in their house. Taylor was in the kitchen. He was finishing the breakfast he had made for himself. Then, it was off to work.

He called up the stairs, "You'll have to fend for yourselves. I gotta go. Why don't you take a morning drive into the country and show Julie what we were up to last night?"

I said, "As soon as I'm awake." It was 9:30 a.m.

The first question she asked, as I slid down the stair railing, was whether we had gone to a bar the night before.

"No," I told her. It was what Taylor had told me to say if she asked.

He'd explained to me months ago what her stance on bars was. "She thinks they're meat markets and that the only reason guys go to them is to find women."

When we went, it was mainly out of boredom, to blow off steam over the dull rituals of everyday life. I talked most of the time. I would try to verbalize my ambiguous plans for the future, while Taylor drank.

Julie stood before me now. I didn't like telling her anything about us. It's a dangerous game to become a married man or woman's confidant. Especially when you start telling lies.

"So, where are we going?" she asked.

"It'll be easier for me to show you than to explain. That is, if I can find it."

She looked at me, puzzled.

Driving to the cemetery in the daylight took the mystery out of last night's trip. We saw the shanties. Toys, garbage, and abandoned cars were strewn through the yards. There were a couple of Gothic farmhouses that had been restored. We passed craters filled with bright blue water at the quarry. If we had crossed the fence there last night, surely we would have wound up swimming.

I found the gravel road and navigated its winding path. It was tamer in the daylight.

Julie was holding onto the shoulder strap of her seatbelt. She asked again, "Where are we going?"

"Just over here," I said, pointing.

She stopped talking when she realized our destination.

I helped her over the fence. We walked through the rows of tombstones and grave markers. Just a hundred yards away, the river was swelling at its banks. I saw now that, at some of the markers, there were shriveled bouquets of flowers and sun-bleached American flags.

"These are the kind of graves you put paper over to get an impression with a charcoal pencil," she said.

"Pretty amazing, huh?"

"So this is what you two did last night. How did you ever find it?"

"Oh, I'd known about it. Guess I read about it in the paper or something. Come here. Look at this one."

At that moment, I'd found a tombstone that was unlike any other there. It was waist-high and chipped away at the edges. The dates read 1892-1894. A child was buried beneath it. That probably explained why it had the impression of a squirrel holding an acorn. I had never seen anything like it.

"We put him in the river, but if the ground could have been broken, this is where he would have gone," I said. I patted the stone with the flat of my palm.

Julie smiled. With her eyes opened wide, she bent down to examine the dates. She couldn't help but feel the relief of the stone animal. When she stood, tears were forming in the corners of her eyes.

She said, "It's beautiful here."

I took her hand in mine. It was cold out.

She looked back once more, as we walked to the car. Then, she stopped and kissed me, the tip of her nose frozen against my cheek.

Christa A. Bergerson

The Melancholic Humor

should I thank him
for raising the dead
now that I'm planning
on saving for my funeral

I want a *nice* coffin
housed within a massive mausoleum
jutting out of the countryside
on top of the highest hill

it will be my citadel
hard and phallic
blanketed in moss
swaddled in verdant life

and there, within the hedgerow
the living will crowd
on bended knees
they'll look upon

a kaleidoscope window
while the lotus opens its mouth
yearning
for ambrosia

B. E. Stock

Brother Thomas' Diagnosis

A colored slide revealed the beautiful tumor
On my neck, its lethal abundance, the way it ravages
The normal flesh. They say I have six months,
If that. A seed sown in the body. Some say,
Another tiny animal, like germs.
I've learned to think asleep. Last night I dreamed
The pain had voices, preaching sacrifice.
I saw the world as a mound of flesh, all

Eating all, alive in another's craw.
I knew immediately what it was:
Life without death. Once there was death,
Eve became the mother of the living.
Could I—in faith He knows my time is over—
Loosen the fist, those unknown levels of rage,
To live and exit like an Indian?
Who is it grabs for immortality,
I or the flesh? If only I could go
Conscious—but that ignores the penalty
Of sin. Only a saint dying daily
Can go directly to His arms, if arms
They be, and not another harsher school.
Ah, to be permanent and solid, know
What I only guess, be what I only strive
To be. That would be worth a martyrdom.
Even, perhaps, slow-cooking sickness,
Blessed words of doom. To make the most
Of what I've managed to collect, fused
In desire, informed by that ecstatic future.
Where's my walker? I'll say my breviary,
Though no one else has time with all the jobs
They've had to take, and I'll be there alone
With no one forced to view my ugliness,

Such as they see it. Any day,
They'll find my body, like a robe removed,
Slung over wood, before that flickering shrine.

Allan Douglass Coleman

Next Life

He imagined the apparent
end might seem almost
like lift-off: All your past
packed up, checked through,
and scanned for whatever should
be left behind; the carry-on,
mere ballast for the soul,
upped odds against the sheer
unlikeliness of flight.

Then pulse of engines, throb
of energy, a forward creeping
to acceleration, gathered speed,
that daring upward tilt,

'til finally the miracle
that no bird questions
more than once or twice.

Speared into cobalt, over
fields of fleece, then leveled,
pointed somewhere that you have
to go. Hold gravity aside.
You're old enough that, from
your early days, you still recall
an invitation to the cockpit,
the kindly pilot urging you
to put your hands on his
at the controls.

But that's for others now;
for you, solicitous attention
to your basic needs. Some
entertainment options—best
of all, a long, slow twilight
for your reveries, a comfortable
pillow for your rest.
From time to time it must
become eventful, he supposed:

Romances and disasters. Make
a new friend or explode
out of the sky. Yet mostly,
it would just feel like
transition. Calm, dark,
dream-deep night. Waking
to the smell of something more
or less like coffee, a hot damp cloth
to wash sleep from your face.

Clean. Breaking fast with bread
and jam. Below you, through
those gaps, is vast water. Dawn
upon the waves. Then, slipping
down beneath the clouds
to no place you will
recognize, back into a body
that can sense deceleration,
and the swift, determined fall
to earth and day:

Not quite impatient, yet
anticipating solid ground.
Prepared to claim some baggage

you have never seen that, strangely,
bears your name. Walk
straight out into the morning
bright with nothing to declare.
Begin where you left off—
wherever that might once
have been, somehow no longer
quite so clear, and fading
rapidly in unfamiliar light.

Melissa Guillet

Token of Faith

An Armenian Chant

If reincarnation be true,
let it be through fire.
Let my bones
be kindling,
stacked like cedar cords
in copper crèches,

where I am reborn, flowing
like the River Styx, forgetting
as I rise, the scarves
of a thousand Moorish dancers;
fireflies, my glowing steps,
a token of faith,
my dirge.

Thoth dips his beak
into an inky sky,
counts every star.

Moon God,
inventor of words:
He speaks, and the words pour out;
his beak, a spout,
his head, an ewer
of language.

When our book closes,
he will weigh our heart,
use wisdom deeper than language
to call out our new name.

Melissa Guillet

Lost Things

The dirge begins,
carried on raindrops,
reflecting yet distorting
all I thought I was.

What is the balance of faith?

The scales are set.
Anubis awaits my heart.

Will my life's good outweigh a feather?

I wait here, without name;
it has been taken from me,
added to the limitless leaves
of the *Tome of Lives*.

How many names have I lost?

After all acts have been inventoried,
after identity is sacrificed,
is there a drop of possibility,
clear and life-giving as water?

Only by forgetting ourselves
can we return,
the skins of possession shed,
to wash the slate clean
and begin again.

David James

A Burning Bush of Sorts

God spoke to me, while I sat alone on the park bench. It was a sunny day in early spring. I could see buds on the trees.

"So, what do you think?" He said.

"About what?"

"All this life busting out around you."

I wouldn't have expected God to say "busting out."

"It's wonderful," I said. "Nice work."

"Do you think there are too many birds? I could cut back on a few species."

"No, not at all. It's the return of the birds that make me think of spring."

For me, the return of the robin is the beginning of spring. My wife says that the first robin around our house is her grandmother, checking in on us. Then, the idea struck me.

"Here's a question for you, God. Is that first robin we see every year our Grandma Ketterer?"

"Oh, I don't know. I'd have to check the inventory, and that takes a while up here."

"But in theory," I said, "do the dead come back to visit us as animals? Or as living things in general?"

"It's possible," He said. "With me, anything is possible, you know."

I thanked him, and ran home to tell my wife the good news.

David James

A Life with Faith

The world sits
in the palm
of my left hand
& knits
my life into yours.
This quiet calm
is heaven,
the breath of an angel
reciting psalms
from the score
of God's imagination.
Sometimes, I close
my eyes and
every worry is undone,
every desire pours
out & grows
into itself, lying
at my feet.
There are those

who ignore
God's signs, crying
for answers,
but I stare
at the darkness, eyeing
a heavenly shore.

David James

A Prayer for the End

The Lord digs in my garden.
I'm tempted to eat the apple.
Under the moon's finger,
I dance like a drunken cat
to the music in my head,
which is not the music God hears.
In the purple night of my final year,
bring me your fire, Lord,
that I might burn away
this doubt and fall toward you.

Ashlee Green and Asa Brown

An Interview with Tim Bascom

Primed with a copy of *Chameleon Days* and a pen, I waited in line to introduce myself to author Tim Bascom. We stood in a congested end room of the University of Pittsburgh's English Department. It was early on a March evening. Bascom had participated in a Writing and Social Responsibility panel discussion. As the minutes passed, I half-expected him to recognize me. After all, I'd read his novel and conducted a telephone interview with him.

Bascom is tall, thin, and lanky. He has a self-assured and fatherly way of welcome. He opened the book with ease and, remembering the spelling of my name, jotted: "Ashlee, thanks for your smart questions and interest in this world."

Perhaps it was the professor in him, always prepped for questions and criticism, or perhaps it was his compassion for the human experience, but Bascom's attention didn't waver as we spoke of life, religion, spirituality, and the complications thereof.

Prior to this evening, I had only met the Timmy Bascom of *Chameleon Days*, the wide-eyed and bushy-tailed youngster who was thrown into Ethiopian culture as the victim of his parents' lofty Christian missionary efforts.

Told from the child's perspective, *Chameleon Days* is an innocent and candid examination of Christian fundamentalism. Raised in the Midwest and transported to a missionary boarding school in Ethiopia, Bascom grew up feeling like a misfit, or with what he calls "third culture kid" identity. While Americans were mourning the death of Martin Luther King, Jr., Bascom was flying kites with Ethiopian boys and idolizing emperor Haile Selassie. While Bascom's parents converted the community, he sat back to question his personal identity and his faith.

Bascom's constant questioning was familiar to me. I'd spent seven years in Catholic school. Not unlike Bascom, I'd spent years exploring an array of religions and philosophies, as I attempted to "pick" a fitting one. I have now become content with the unknown. I am unperturbed by my own curiosity. I identify as an agnostic, and I have realized over time, that this too is a legitimate creed.

It's astounding how experience at a young age molds one's life-long conscience. Bascom offers his life as literary proof.

Interviewer: There's a strong religious overtone in *Chameleon Days*. Did you get flak for that? How did you avoid coming off as a fundamentalist or preachy?

Tim Bascom: People react when they feel that something is being imposed on them. I try just to tell my story, letting you know what I felt—what I went through—as opposed to saying, "This is what you ought to do." We tend to listen to other people's experiences open-mindedly if we don't feel that they're supposed to be a blueprint for the way we should live.

The other thing I'm hoping is that, here and there, people sense that I am not completely sold on some of the theology that was given to me as a child. In quiet ways, I'm critiquing that way of thinking. Because this critique comes from a child's point of view, it's not overt. It's not like a commentary on fundamentalism.

There are kind of subtle, quiet ways in which this happens. I'm thinking of the chapter about the lake—Lake Bishoftu, where we go out on the water as a family. I think it's pretty evident that the child prefers to be together as a family on the Sabbath, as opposed to being stuck indoors and listening to a sermon in a traditional religious way.

It's sharing those kinds of experiences that also probably makes the reader feel comfortable—the reader who's not so sure about fundamentalist religion.

Interviewer: You mentioned the child's perspective. I noticed that the use of this in *Chameleon Days* allowed you to be a little bit vulnerable. However, some people have said that a child's narrative can be unreliable. Did you feel that you were unreliable at any point?

Bascom: That's interesting. I'm sure it can be. So can an adult's. A child never understands everything and so is unreliable in that sense. Of course, adults don't either. They just think they do. On the other hand, a child is often very honest in a way that may be more reliable than some adults who have reason or agenda for not giving the full scoop. I felt like, for the most part, assuming that identity, or that stage in life, helped me to be more honest as opposed to less.

I did struggle with the limits of that point of view—not knowing a lot about adult realities—and that was difficult. I tried to learn what I could, for starters. I had experienced all of it as a child, so I really didn't know, even as an adult, some of the things that had occurred or what the dynamics were behind them. I had to go and interview my parents, talk to other people, read books to fill in gaps. Then I had to find ways to weave that in, and, to be honest, it's the place where I've become more creative and less nonfiction.

There are some places where there are conversations that I probably never did hear as a child, but I did hear them later in life. I've integrated them into my childhood experience, because, in fact, that makes the story more reliable, even though I am in a way doing a sleight of hand. It's kind of odd, because I'm being more reliable, but I'm playing a trick on the reader. For instance, when I crawl out of bed, come down the hall, and hear my mother saying to my father, "I feel like I'm failing here as a missionary." I never did that. But I did, in my research, read a very personal letter— kind of like a journal entry—in which she said that very thing. In fact, she recorded a conversation between the two of them. So I'm taking that conversation and putting it into the story, as if I'd overheard it, because I'm trying to stay true to that child's point of view.

Interviewer: Being immersed in a missionary-kids-only school, do you in any way feel that you weren't given the chance to experience full-fledged Ethiopian culture when you were a child?

Bascom: I have to be difficult and ask you, as you read it, did you feel that way?

Interviewer: Well… in a way.

Bascom: That's why I'm asking. Yeah, I did not get to experience Ethiopian culture fully. Some of that was because of the mission school. I think missionary children who get sent off to school like that do tend to be cut off from the culture. Even when you're at home, you're on a compound typically—or we were in that era. Things have changed somewhat now. Then, that compound was kind of its own little island. It's necessary, because you're not entirely equipped to be Ethiopian. I would say almost anybody, even as much as they try to be integrated, is not going to get fully into a culture unless they marry into it, have children.

I was trying to let people know that I wasn't in fully. I find myself embarrassed by that somewhat, looking back. I, as a younger person, thought that I knew a lot about Ethiopia, but in fact I feel like that was one of the sadnesses of it—that I couldn't be more integrated.

Interviewer: Even as a child, it seemed that you were aware of Haile Selassie's cultural and emblematic status. Could you expand a bit more on the heroic portrayal you gave him in the book?

Bascom: To the missionaries as a subculture in Ethiopia, Haile Selassie was highly regarded. He was one of the last kings, or emperors, and he had sort of foretold World War II. When Italy occupied Ethiopia and he was overthrown, there was general dismay. The missionaries felt that he was sympathetic to Christianity. He seemed to have been supportive. He had given land to the mission in different places for the stations. As a child, I was, of course, going to see him from the point of view of my parents and the mission. So, he was nothing but a heroic figure for me.

The other thing is that Western nations found him fascinating. After he was forced out of Ethiopia, he went to the United Nations and said, "Watch out, because this thing is just going to grow." He turned out to be kind of prophetic. When he was helped back into the country by the English, I think Americans and the British fell in love with him, as a figure who was seen as both a reformer and a modern leader. He helped start what's now called the Organization of African Unity. He was really highly regarded.

It was only in his later life, when there were popular uprisings, that, apparently, he was so disconnected from his own people that he didn't recognize or admit all the suffering that was going on during the famine. He was even trying to shut reporters out and not let them report on what was happening. As a result, tens of thousands of people were dying without help. That's when his government finally lost its support, and the Marxist revolution occurred.

It's only later, as an adult, that I can look at him and say that he was probably greedy—that he was probably cruel in some sense. But I think, even now, I find myself more supportive of him than perhaps some who would be quick to critique him. I think he was a relatively benign—a relatively successful ruler of the sort he was. Finally, though, there wasn't much room for that kind of leadership at that point in history.

We don't think much of kings now. There's something natural, however, about children being drawn to that kind of leader. If you think about it, girls are always wanting to be princesses in fairy tales, and I think boys want to be king. From the child's point of view, there's a natural attraction—even if it's misguided.

Interviewer: As a child, did you feel more Ethiopian than American?

Bascom: I wouldn't say that I felt more Ethiopian. As I was saying, I was not as connected to Ethiopian culture as I thought I was. But, researchers have found that, oftentimes, people who live in other cultures are surprised to have a harder time returning to their own culture than they did going to the new culture. They call it "reverse culture shock."

I think I was going through "reverse culture shock" when we returned to Kansas. What happens is this. You think you know about your home culture, and you still feel that that's where you belong. But now you've been changed irrevocably by what you've been through. You don't fit in the way that you used to. You've started to adopt some of the values and ways of thinking of that other culture in a way that makes it very hard to feel comfortable in the home culture.

Researchers have come up with a term for missionary kids, military kids, and children of diplomats. People who've had to travel a lot and live in other cultures are sometimes called "third culture kids." What it means is that, after being shifted around numerous times, the young person doesn't belong to one culture or the other, but has kind of a third culture. This is a culture that's kind of cosmopolitan and not rooted. Maybe the place where that person will feel most comfortable is on an airplane with a lot of travelers—with people who see the world through cultural lenses. That is another reason why coming back to the U.S. was not as easy as I would've expected.

Interviewer: Do you feel that your self-described "cosmopolitan" childhood shaped your travel writing and your career to this day?

Bascom: Sure. I think it becomes so much a part of yourself that it's in everything without even thinking about it. It's just instinctive. The way that I go through life—which I find difficult at times—is by looking in two directions at once, because I'm thinking comparatively. It slows me down.

The chameleon has eyes that spin two directions and look at two different hemispheres. That makes it a clumsy creature. It feels like a curse at times not to go with the flow, but, on the other hand, it's a gift. It naturally leads to wanting to write, to express insights about those differences or similarities. The travel writing is a natural extension of that point of view.

In terms of career, as a teacher as well, I tend to love teaching stories and poems that have a border-crossing feel to them. Pieces about ethnic minorities here in the United States, or about people who are negotiating two cultures at once. Travelers who go into other places, that kind of thing.

Interviewer: We've been reading a lot about the theme of travel as spiritual transcendence. Is that what you were going for in *Chameleon Days*? Did changing locations lead to epiphanies of any sort?

Bascom: I don't think that I was intentionally trying to pursue that with the book as a whole. The book has a kind of religious backdrop. I see it as being more about a family and what happens to a family under cultural stress. These epiphanies— I don't think they're something that I've intentionally sought out. At this point in my life, though, I am more conscious of what happens with travel. There's a reason that people go on pilgrimages. That pilgrimage is an attempt to get kicked out of your comfort zone and, by traveling, to open yourself up spiritually.

I like to compare myself to our cat. If we take him on a trip, he hates it. He's in the car and very nervously crying the whole way. You stop at a rest area and let him out, and he is extremely anxious. He's on a leash, because if he's not, we're going to lose him completely. He's in unfamiliar territory, so he's on high alert. It's not that there's always fear connected with travel, but there is some.

The fear itself awakens your senses and puts you on high alert. I think that's part of the reason you have these transcendent moments. Basically, you're not asleep like you normally are when you're going through an ordinary day, and so things happen. You start seeing things you hadn't seen before. You start feeling things you hadn't felt before. You're open and receptive in a way you haven't been. That leads to these epiphanies. Some people become travel junkies, because they think they get a high with it. For a while, I think I was. Now I've been working harder at getting my feet down on the ground here in the Midwest and staying connected, which has been good too.

Interviewer: There's a point in *Chameleon Days* that chronicles your early conversion attempt—when you asked your mother to help you pray to be saved. Did that serve as a formative experience or influence your cultural outlook?

Bascom: Sure. I felt a little awkward writing about it, knowing how some would react, but I felt that to be a truth I had to tell. For my childhood, that was a demarcation between Tim who wasn't saved and Tim who was saved. I put a lot of weight on it.

In evangelical churches, I think the heavy weight that's placed on a conversion experience means that there's a kind of blindness to how much of the spiritual life is a process. There's this desire for things to be immediately fixed—to have one moment of blinding light, and have everything be changed. In fact I think all the evidence points to the contrary. For most of us at least, spiritual experience is a process. It happens slowly. People change over time.

I told that story, but I think it has in it subtle hints that I'm going to be dissatisfied. By the end of the conversion prayer, I'm already saying, "Why don't I feel Jesus inside my heart? Why don't I feel physically different? Why isn't there something expanding in my chest? Why isn't there evidence of this radical change that I've been led to believe would occur?"

By hinting at that dissatisfaction, I think I'm quietly letting the reader know that this may not be all that it's cut out to be. It may not be the cure-all that people make it seem to be.

You were asking earlier, "How can I avoid falling into the trap of seeming preachy?" That's a case and point of honestly letting the reader know the failings in the religious teaching I was being given.

Interviewer: I noticed that you taught at Simpson College in Iowa— originally a Methodist school that still has an affiliation with the Methodist church. Do you think that teaching in a secular environment would marginalize some of the overarching themes in *Chameleon Days*? Would you approach teaching in the same way for both secular and religious universities? Do you feel that you'd be more easily attacked in a secular environment?

Bascom: When your audience shares a similar religious upbringing, there's a new comfort level you can have about discussing prayer, conversion, church, and the things that go with that life. I enjoyed that. I also felt a little bit challenged to be prophetic. Also, to talk about what I felt wasn't so good in the church upbringing that I had, at least a little bit, as a warning for people to be careful about certain things.

I think things are changing. When I was a graduate student at the University of Kansas twenty years ago, you did not talk about your Christian experience in public, or you risked ridicule and ostracism. I remember talking with a professor I was just meeting. He was being extremely critical of Christians and Christianity as a whole, at which point I told him, "You ought to know I'm a Christian." He was really taken aback. He kind of backpedaled.

I'd thought, "I can't just sit here and let him do this and have integrity, quietly let him butcher the faith that has been mine." I let him know that. I think it was a half of a year later that he wrote me a note saying that if I ever needed a reference, he'd be glad to write it. I think he saw me very differently.

At that time I felt I had to be in the closet as a Christian in an academic environment. However, now, the very fact that I'm invited to Pittsburgh to talk on this subject is evidence of a new receptivity towards people's talking about their spiritual experience. For some reason, I think people are just more open on a broad level to discussion of spirituality. I've had essays that were pretty frank about spiritual matters published in literary journals. I don't think that they would ever have been published twenty years ago.

Interviewer: Do you feel that your faith shapes or informs your writing? Are there ever any conflicts of interest—does it ever hinder your ability to publish?

Bascom: Yes, that's been a tension I've felt a lot as I've been working on things. I've felt it less lately. I've felt there's been more openness. I think that's partly because I've changed in the way that I write about my spirituality, even in the use of the term "spiritual." The way I think about it is quite broad now. I would welcome discussion with people about their experience that might be quite different from mine. Coming out of a different religious tradition, for instance, or coming out of no religious tradition. I feel that people who are atheists have a valid point of view and are going to also have spiritual experience. They would insist that they do as well.

For me, it's about the alertness we were talking about with the cat. It doesn't have to come from fear. It's just that there are moments in life when, for one reason or another, we are highly aware and centered. We feel connected to others, to the world, to nature. Those moments are the ones characterized as spiritual. They are often accompanied by some sense of epiphany—having seen something that we couldn't before. People of all faiths and people who don't want to be associated with religious faith have those experiences.

I feel increasingly comfortable in that arena, just to be part of that discussion. I've changed enough that I don't have that same tension in me when I walk into a room to talk about such things. I don't intend to convert people. For one thing, I really like people who are different from me, including the ones who believe differently than I do. It's paradoxical: I was raised to think that if they believe differently, then I have to change them. I don't feel that same conflict that I would've as a young person.

Interviewer: In a 1998 piece about freelance writing, you wrote, "I have eighty articles in print, plus two books and a dozen poems. But after years of trying to make a living as a freelance writer, I now admit I probably will never succeed." Now, ten years later, with the wide reception of *Chameleon Days* and being awarded with the Bakeless Literary Prize, do you feel you have succeeded?

Bascom: I feel good about the Bakeless Prize and the book's being published. I think I was more driven to be successful earlier. Now, I have more of a desire to be successful just so that I can keep writing. I just want to write. Well, that's not entirely true. I want people to read what I write. I feel fulfilled when others receive it and respond. That, for me, is the ultimate satisfaction.

These moments when you get an award are important in the sense that they help to make more writing possible. I don't feel satisfied yet, and I probably never will.

I feel blocked a lot of the time on getting to write more. I don't make enough money from what I publish to do it as much as I want. It's that kind of thing that's hard.

The other thing about the whole awards system—particularly in literary journals and circles—is that it gets really competitive. It's like the Olympics for writers. With that comes jealousy. It comes even when you're succeeding. Honestly, in my case, because I'm a flawed person, I'm going to get jealous. I don't have a sense of having arrived, if that's what you're wondering. I'm going to look over and see somebody who's doing better. That can create distraction and distress.

Generally, the solution to that kind of thought or distraction is to just quit thinking about them and do the best you can. Given what I've got, I write as much as I can and do as well as I can.

Carlos Ponce-Meléndez

Good News from the Future

The rich people of the world agreed to share their wealth with the poor, said the newspaper today. The following news was about the transformation of the last two weapons factories into technical schools. The reason for the change: Lack of sales.

A three-fold increase in the budget for research was, again, the news in science. The money will be used to find the cure for the last epidemic on earth and to fund research in quality of life for the general population.

The Metro section said that the last five policemen had been fired, as well as all judges, due to the lack of crime in the city for the past seven years running. According to the paper, our city was just following the world trend.

In economics the big deal was that pharmaceutical companies had discovered that a small profit margin yielded higher earnings. Real estate moguls and automakers had reached the same conclusion several years back.

In sports, the news of the day was that all professional leagues were being dissolved to create amateur championships that would play for the love of the game. Children and senior citizens would be encouraged to join.

The Society pages were filled with stories of new clubs that are dedicated to cultural and charitable endeavors, the only difficulty being that these organizations have to compete for the same public interest.

The lead story in the Entertainment section said that new movies are tremendously successful because they are artistic and not violent. Theater, music, and video games are undergoing similar transformation.

No, this is not a dream. We will get there.

Contributors' Notes

CARL ALESSI is a self-taught writer and artist. Recently, his poems and stories have appeared in *Chiron Review*, *Outlaw Poetry Journal*, *Big Hammer*, and *Songs of Innocence*. His artwork has appeared on twelve covers of *Blue Beat Jacket*. His art has appeared in two group shows put on by Art Enables in Washington, D.C. Much of his work is inspired by dreams.

ADRIENNE AMUNDSEN is a psychologist in San Francisco and San Rafael, California. She works mainly with early trauma. She is married and the mother of two boys. Born and raised in Texas, she made it to the West Coast in time for the tumultuous and amazing sixties. In addition to her therapy practice, she has a horse, teaches classes on Paleolithic cave art and shamanism, and tries to stay politically active. Her writing influences include Barbara Kingsolver, Margaret Atwood, Rumi, Jim Morrison, and U2.

BARRY BALLARD'S poetry has recently appeared in *Prairie Schooner*, the *Connecticut Review*, *Margie*, and *Puerto del Sol*. His most recent collection is *A Body Speaks Through Fence Lines* (Pudding House, 2006). He writes from Burleson, Texas. (abballard@hotmail.com)

TIM BASCOM'S memoir *Chameleon Days* (Mariner Books, 2006) won the Bakeless Literary Prize. He has also won editor's prizes for his essays printed in the *Missouri Review* and the *Florida Review*, and has been published in *Best American Travel Writing*. His earlier publications include a novel titled *Squatters' Rites* (New Day Press, 1990) and a collection of essays, *The Comfort Trap: Spiritual Dangers of a Convenience Culture* (InterVarsity Press, 1993). Mr. Bascom is a graduate of the Nonfiction Writing Program at the University of Iowa. He lives in Des Moines, Iowa.

CHRISTA A. BERGERSON'S intuited metaphysical work has appeared in *Candor*, *Quantum Pulp*, and *Open Ways*, and is forthcoming in *Faerie Nation* magazine. She is a defender of Nature and all of her wondrous inhabitants, even those that writhe betwixt the veil. In the twilight hours she finds pleasure traversing the wilds of Illinois. She dreams of life beyond borders, space, and time.

ASA BROWN is a National Merit Scholar. He was awarded an academic scholarship to the University of Pittsburgh, where he majored in nonfiction and legal studies. He now plans to pursue a J.D./M.B.A. from Cornell University. He is also a Series-7 certified day trader.

WENDY BROWN is a performance poet who has appeared throughout the United States and Mexico; in cafes, bars, bookstores, galleries, peace centers, and private homes; solo and in collaborations. In 2004, she released a poetry CD called *Longing for Home* and created a bilingual ensemble piece. Her poetry and creative nonfiction have appeared in various literary magazines, including *Borderlands*, *A Texas Poetry Review*, *Sin Fronteras*, *Out of Line*, the *Litchfield Review*, and the *Chrysalis Reader*. Her latest novel is *MoonSense* (Creatrix Books, 2008), a spiritual parable about an ancient tribe who worship the Moon Goddess.

Ms. Brown is also the creator of Writing Circles for Healing, a writing support group to heal loss, grief, illness, and other life-altering experiences: www.writingcirclesforhealing.com.

"Why do I love poetry? Because it cracks open the darkness. Because the audience holds me in the grip of their hearts."

RICHARD ALAN BUNCH is the author of *Wading the Russian River* (Norton Coker Press, 1993), *Sacred Space* (Dry Bones Press, 1998), and *Running for Daybreak* (Mellen Press, 2004). His poems have been translated into Japanese, Hindi, and Italian. His poetry has appeared in *Timber Creek Review*, *Cape Rock*, *Hawai'i Review*, *Black Mountain Review*, *California Quarterly*, *Poetry New Zealand*, *Orbis*, and the *Oregon Review*.

JANINE CANAN is a California-based psychiatrist, award-winning author, and longtime Amma devotee. Her books include a collection of short stories, *Journeys with Justine* (Regent Press, 2007); *Goddesses, Goddesses: Essays* (Regent Press, 2007); *Walk Now in Beauty: The Legend of Changing Woman* (Regent Press, 2007); and *In the Palace of Creation: Selected Works 1969-1999* (Scars Publications, 2003). Janine also edited *Messages from Amma: In the Language of the Heart* (Celestial Arts, 2004) and *She Rises like the Sun: Invocations of the Goddess by Contemporary American Women Poets* (The Crossing Press, 1989). She has translated *Star in My Forehead* (Holy Cow! Press, 2000), a collection of poetry by Else Lasker-Schüler, and a forthcoming book by Francis Jammes, *Under the Azure*.

ALLAN DOUGLASS COLEMAN has published eight books and more than two thousand essays on photography and related subjects. Formerly a columnist for the *Village Voice*, the *New York Times*, and the *New York Observer*, Coleman now contributes to *ARTnews*, *Art on Paper*, and *Technology Review*. His syndicated essays on mass media, new communication technologies, art, and photography are featured in such periodicals as *Juliet Art Magazine* (Italy), *European Photography* (Germany), and *La Fotografia* (Spain). His fiction and poetry have appeared in *Nimrod, Cross Currents, International Poetry Review, Sanskrit,* and others.

Mr. Coleman lectures worldwide and has appeared on NPR, PBS, CBS, and the BBC. He is a Fulbright Senior Scholar and recipient of grants from the National Endowment for the Arts and the Hasselblad Foundation. He serves as publisher and executive director of the electronic magazine *Nearby Café* (www.nearbycafe.com).

M. L. CORDLE is the author of *Silencing Sarah* (Resplendence Publishing, 2007). She realized that she might be well on her way to establishing a readership when she was offered an interview with Angela MackIntosh, the CEO of the monthly publication, *Women on Writing*. Since then, Ms. Cordle has acquired the endorsement of *New York Times* best-selling author, Adriana Trigiani, who offered a blurb to go on the cover of the book.

Ms. Cordle's work can be viewed in literary journals such as *Origami Condom*, the *California Quarterly*, and *Tertulia Magazine*. She freelances occasionally for *Women on Writing*. Her second suspense novel is *Breach of Trust* (Wild Child Publishing, 2008).

ORMAN DAY, a resident of Durham, North Carolina, is writing a book about his backpacking travels through ninety countries and the fifty states. His short stories, essays, and poetry have been published by such literary journals as *Zyzzyva*, *Creative Nonfiction*, *Inkwell*, *William & Mary Review*, *Color Wheel*, *Bitter Oleander*, and *Alembic*.

DEBORAH DeNICOLA'S fifth poetry collection is *Inside Light* (Finishing Line Press, 2007). She is also the author of a spiritual memoir *The Alchemy of the Black Madonna & the Future That Brought Her Here* (Nicolas-Hays Press, 2008). She has edited anthologies including *Orpheus & Company: Contemporary Poems on Greek Mythology* (University Press of New England, 1999) and *Where Divinity Begins* (Alice James Books, 1994).

CORRINE DE WINTER is the author of seven collections of poetry and prose, including *The Women at the Funeral* (Space & Time Press, 2004), which won the 2004 Bram Stoker Award for superior achievement in poetry, and *Tango in the Ninth Circle* (Dark Regions Press, 2007). She was nominated twice for the Pushcart Prize. Ms. De Winter's poetry, fiction, essays, and interviews have appeared worldwide in publications such as the *New York Quarterly*, *Imago*, *Phoebe*, *Plainsongs*, *Yankee*, *Sacred Journey*, *Interim*, the *Chrysalis Reader*, the *Lucid Stone*, *Fate*, *Press*, *Sulphur River Literary Review*, *Modern Poetry*, the *Lyric*, *Atom Mind*, the *Writer*, and more than eight hundred other publications. She has been the recipient of awards from Triton College of Arts & Sciences and *Writer's Digest*. She has also been the recipient of the Esme Bradberry Award, the Madeline Sadin Award, the Rhysling Award, and has been featured in *Poet's Market*. Ms. De Winter is a resident of Massachusetts.

CAROL EMSHWILLER grew up in Ann Arbor, Michigan and France. She has written six novels and five short story collections. Her latest books are *The Secret City* (2007), a novel, and a short story collection called *I Live With You* (2005), both from Tachyon Publications. She has received a National Endowment for the Arts grant, two New York State Foundation for the Arts grants, and two World Fantasy awards.

JOHN FITZPATRICK received Vermont Studio Center poetry residencies in 2002 and 2004. He is also the recipient of the 2003 Hackney Poetry Literary Award from Birmingham-Southern College, and honors in *City Works, Mad Poets Review, Confluence, Taproot Literary Review,* and *Clark College 2004 Writers.* His poetry has been published or is forthcoming in the *Yalobusha Review,* the *Mid-America Poetry Review, California Quarterly, Luna Negra,* the *Cape Rock, Plainsongs, SLAB, Out of Line, Snow Monkey,* the *Rock River Times, ICON, Common Ground Review, Chronogram,* and others.

Mr. Fitzpatrick was born in the Genesee River Valley village of Dansville, New York, the home of Clara Barton and her first American Red Cross Chapter. He now lives in the Hudson River Valley village of Red Hook, which is known for its progressive policies to save the region's scenic beauty. Growing up, he frequently roamed the woods on his maternal Schmidt grandparents' farm; now, he tries to talk to trees and plants and listens more carefully to what they have to tell him.

BRETT GADBOIS has written short stories, songs, and a novel. Besides writing, his favorite activities include spending time with his red-headed ball-of-fire nine-year-old boy, working on his rock garden, and sitting Zen meditation. His fiction has been published in *Out of Line, Colere,* the *MacGuffin, Short Stories Bimonthly, PINYON,* and *Exhibition.* His nonfiction has appeared in *Streams.* He is currently writing a children's book for his son.

ASHLEE GREEN grew up in rural Pennsylvania and attended Catholic middle school. Questioning organized religion, she transferred to public school in the eighth grade. There, she began identifying herself as an agnostic, studying world religions independently, and practicing yoga. She is currently majoring in creative nonfiction at the University of Pittsburgh, where she is a staff writer for both the Pittsburgh arts and culture magazine the *Original* and the student newspaper's Arts and Entertainment section. This summer she will travel to India to study at the University of Hyderabad. She enjoys writing about the health of mind and body. She hopes to become a Vinyasa Yoga instructor following graduation.

JOHN GREY is an Australian-born poet, playwright, and musician. His latest book is *What Else Is There* (Main Street Rag, 2004). His recent publications include the *English Journal*, the *Pedestal*, *Pearl*, and the *Journal of the American Medical Association*.

MELISSA GUILLET'S work has appeared in various literary magazines and anthologies, including *Bleeding on the Page*, the *Cherry Blossom Review*, *Nth Position*, *Scrivener's Pen*, *Six Worcester*, *MA Anthologies*, and other collections. She is a member of Dr. Brown's Traveling Poetry Troupe and teaches Interdisciplinary Arts in East Providence, Rhode Island.

FLORENCE HOMOLKA'S writings have been published in *Fiction International*, *Big Sky Journal*, the *New York Quarterly*, the *NC Review*, and others. She is also a meditation teacher and sacred musician. She is an editor of *Lalitamba*.

PAUL HOSTOVSKY'S poems appear widely online and in print. He has been featured in *Poetry Daily*, *Verse Daily*, and the *Writer's Almanac*. He has published two chapbooks, *Bird in the Hand* (Grayson Books, 2006) and *Dusk Outside the Braille Press* (Riverstone Press, 2006). He works in Boston as a sign language interpreter. To read more of Paul's poetry, visit his website: www.paulhostovsky.com.

SHINJO ITO (1906-1989) was born on March 28, 1906 in Yamanashi, Japan. He showed extraordinary artistic talent as a child and went on to study photography and to win awards for his work. At the same time, Shinjo Ito was drawn towards spirituality. Eventually, he gave up his job as an engineer to enter Kyoto's Daigoji monastery, the head temple of the Daigo school of Shingon Buddhism, one of Japan's oldest denominations. There, he attained the rank of Grand Master. Even after Shinjo Ito and his followers established the order of Shinnyo-en, art continued to be an integral part of Shinjo Ito's religious pursuit. He sculpted and photographed throughout his life. The cover art is "Kotobuki," which translates as "Felicitations."

DAVID JAMES' books of poems include *A Heart Out of This World* (Carnegie Mellon University Press, 1984), and four others from March Street Press: *Do Not Give Dogs What Is Holy* (1994), *I Dance Back* (2002), *I Will Peel This Mask Off* (2004), and *Trembling in Someone's Palm* (2007). His one-act plays have been produced off-Broadway. He teaches for Oakland Community College.

MAGGIE JOCHILD of Austin, Texas received the Loving Lesbians Poetry Award from the Astraea Lesbian Writer's Fund in 2002 and again in 2005. She is a creative writing workshop facilitator for the Finding Voice Production Series developed by Sharon Bridgforth. She is a sixth-generation Texan, a mother, a grandmother, and a godmother. Her recent publication credits include *Natural Bridge, Asphodel, Texas Poetry Calendar 2006, Rockhurst Review, Bridges,* and *Albatross.* She has also been included in several anthologies, including *Di-Verse-City 2006* (the Austin International Poetry Festival anthology).

BHAU KALCHURI: It is difficult to find, in the introductions to Bhau's more than twenty books, much about him personally. One can be sure that was his preference. As he wrote in *Meher Sarod* (Manifestation, 1984), "These *ghazals* are the gift of Beloved Baba; the arrows of His glance struck my heart and awakened me to compose them. While depending fully on the Beloved, my helplessness received this *prasad* from Him, which is now before the reader."

Bhau, as Meher Baba's servant and disciple, has done extraordinary work, while escaping much personal notice. He has written plays, poems, songs, *ghazals*, and ultimately, Meher Baba's six-thousand-page biography, all at Baba's order.

Before dedicating his life to Baba, Bhau had never considered himself a writer. Bhau completed his masters degrees in law, chemistry, and public administration. In 1953, at age twenty-six, just as he was finishing his law degree, he met Meher Baba. A great longing was stirred in him. He left all to join Baba and serve Him, which he does to this day at age eighty-two.

Bhau lives in Ahmednagar, India, near Meherabad, the place where Meher Baba lived and worked, and the location of His tomb. Bhau's wife and two children came under the care of Meher Baba when Bhau joined Him. Bhau's children and grandchildren remain devoted to Baba, some at Meherabad and some in the United States.

Bhau is now the Chairman of the Avatar Meher Baba Trust, a nonprofit trust that funds and operates hospitals, clinics, schools, and agricultural learning centers for the poor in India. In addition to maintaining Meher Baba's Tomb Shrine as a place of pilgrimage, Bhau manages daily business at the trust office. He guides and inspires disciples of Meher Baba, who visit Baba's home from all around the world, by telling stories of his life with Meher Baba and sharing and explaining Baba's thought. He communicates internationally, most recently through Internet chats. He has also traveled as far as the United States, Australia, and Europe, meeting with young and old alike who wish to taste of that wine which Meher Baba poured so generously for Bhau. Of Baba's *Mandali*, Bhau is one of the few remaining living disciples and is infinitely precious to Baba lovers, near and far.

If Bhau has been anonymous in some ways, it is because he became lost in the Beloved as was his wont. Adi K. Irani, in his introduction to *Meher Geetika* (Companion Enterprises, 1986), says that these songs "though they pertain to [Bhau's] own experiences, do not belong exclusively to him. They belong to anyone who cares to read, recite, and sing—drawing from them the truths, morals, and advice, and above all, the love blessings of Meher Baba, who inspired Bhau to write."

RICK KEMPA lives in Rock Springs, Wyoming, where he directs the honors program at Western Wyoming College. His poems and essays have recently appeared in *Bellowing Ark*, *Cream City Review*, the *Healing Muse*, *Pilgrimage*, *Puerto del Sol*, *Redivider*, and elsewhere.

BEN KOCH is a writer and teacher in the Dallas area. He's most recently been published in *Highlights for Children*, *Transitions Abroad*, and *Zampa*, a publication of Karma Triyana Dharmachakra, a Buddhist monastery in Woodstock, New York. He's also very proud to have served as editor for the book *Falling Off the Roof of the World: The Autobiography of the Venerable Lama Dudjom Dorjee* (Infinity Publishing, 2006). He can be reached at benjasereni@yahoo.com.

P. KOBYLARZ'S recent work appears or will appear in the *Iconoclast, Visions International, New American Writing, Slab, Poetry, Salzburg Review,* and is included in *Best American Poetry 2007.*

W. K. LAWRENCE has published poems, stories, and nonfiction in various literary magazines, journals, anthologies, and newspapers, both in print and online. His first collection of poetry, titled *State of Love and Trust,* was published in 2005 by True Step Press. Gray Horse Press recently published a chapbook of his environmental poems titled *Breathe.*

REBECCA LILLY is the author of two poetry collections: *You Want to Sell Me a Small Antique* (Gibbs Smith, 2002), which was the winner of the Peregrine Smith Poetry Prize, and a book of haiku, *Shadwell Hills* (Birch Brook Press, 2002). Her poems have recently appeared in the *Iowa Review* and *International Poetry Review.*

KIRK LUMPKIN is the author of two books of poetry, *In Deep* (Zyga Multimedia Research, 2004) and *Co-Hearing* (Zyga Multimedia Research, 1983). His magazine publications include *Alternate Routes* (both a written piece and a recording of two poetry/music pieces), *Am Here Forum, City Miner* magazine, the *Croton Review, Earth First!* journal, *Green Fuse, Heaven Bone, Poetsagainstthewar.org, Poetalk, Salthouse, Shattersheet,* the *Telluride Watch, Temenos, Terrain, There It Is* magazine, *Third Lung Review* (3rd place OXFAM Poetry Contest), *Verve, Wordgathering.org,* and others.

As a solo poet he has performed throughout the San Francisco Bay Area and Northern California. He formerly hosted the San Francisco Bay Guardian Winner for Best Spoken Word Open Mic. He has also appeared at Beyond Baroque in Los Angeles and at the Bowery Poetry Club in New York City, as well as in Colorado, Canada, and Great Britain.

Mr. Lumpkin has been a Pirate Radio DJ. He is the founder of The Word-Music Continuum (poetry/music band) that will soon release its second CD, *Sound Poems*. He recently released an album of original rock songs, *Moondog Sessions*, and is a vocalist with the Wild Buds.

He is also on the board of PEN Oakland. He works for the Ecology Center as the Special Events and Promotions Coordinator of the Berkeley Farmers' Markets.

JULIE MARS is a teacher of English, a writer, a certified yoga instructor, a working hypnotist, a meditator, a fairly accomplished tile-guy, and an all-around bon vivant. She has made it to age fifty-seven more or less intact and considers herself one of the lucky people whose life has gotten better as time piled on. She is the author of *Anybody Any Minute* (a novel published by St. Martin's Press in 2008), *A Month of Sundays: Searching for the Spirit, My Sister* (a memoir, and finalist for the Independent Press Memoir of the Year, published by GreyCore Press in 2005), and *The Secret Keepers* (GreyCore Press, 2000). A Barnes & Noble "Discover Great New Writers" author, she has also received a grant from the New York Foundation of the Arts and a New Jersey Arts Council Grant in Fiction (among others). Julie is a widely published freelance journalist. She holds an M.A. in Creative Writing from the City University of New York.

JANET MCCANN was born in 1942. Journals publishing her poems include *Kansas Quarterly, Parnassus, Nimrod, Sou'wester, Christian Century, Christianity and Literature*, the *New York Quarterly, Tendril, Poetry Australia*, and *McCall's*, among many others. Her latest book is *Looking for Buddha in the Barbed Wire Garden* (Avisson, 1996). She has won three chapbook contests, sponsored by Pudding Publications, Chimera Connections, and Franciscan University Press. A 1989 NEA Creative Writing Fellowship winner, Ms. McCann has taught at Texas A & M University since 1969, where she was coordinator of the creative writing department until recently, and is currently a professor of English.

JUSTIN R. MCMANUS: "I started writing when I was in high school. I first started writing because I played the guitar a little bit and had ideas of starting my own band, in which case we would need our own songs. Well, I never started a band, but I continued to write. I was on the quiet side and never told anyone about my writing. I kept it a secret from family and friends. Over the years I have filled notebooks and numerous pieces of scrap paper with my thoughts and ideas. A few lines here and a few more there. I am now twenty-seven years old. I work as a teacher. Most of the themes that I write about are love, lost love, feeling like you don't fit in, isolation, faith, religion, and trying to find out who you are. I feel that most of my themes are universal. I write as a way to put my thoughts and feelings down on paper, to try and figure out this riddle we call life. Poets who inspire my writing include Poe, Hughes, Wilde, Frost, Dickinson, and Thomas."

CARLOS PONCE-MELÉNDEZ'S poetry has appeared or is forthcoming in *Small Brushes*, *Arch and Quiver*, the *Poet*, *Karamu*, the *Texas Observer*, *Voices Along the River*, *Reforma*, *Attention*, *Blue Collar Review*, and the *Express News*, among others. He is also the author of a collection of short stories and two children books.

BOBBY MINKOFF, PH.D. is a licensed psychologist in private practice and a professor of psychology and human services. He is also a storyteller and a member of the National Storytelling Association.

A. J. NASLUND has enjoyed a career as a university English professor, teaching in the United States, in Japan, and in South Korea. The writer has academic degrees from the University of Montana (Missoula, Montana—B.A. and M.A.) and the University of Louisville (Ph.D.). His work has appeared or will appear in such journals as *Upstreet*, *Abiko Annual* (Japan), *Caesura*, *Lips*, *Ceramics Monthly*, *Kentucky Poetry Review*, the *Louisville Review*, and others. He is the author of a book of poems, *Silk Weather* (Fleur-de-lis Press, 1999). The poet's other interests include writing drama and fiction, and throwing pots. A resident of Louisville, Kentucky, Naslund grew up on a farm in Montana in the forties and fifties.

NANCY OWEN NELSON has published articles in academic journals and anthologies. She is co-editor of *The Selected Letters of Frederick Manfred: 1932-1954* (University of Nebraska Press, 1989). She is the editor of *Private Voices, Public Lives: Women Speak on the Literary Life* (University of North Texas Press, 1995) and *The Lizard Speaks: Essays on the Writings of Frederick Manfred* (The Center for Western Studies, 1998). Her poems have been published in the anthology *What Wildness Is This?* (University of Texas Press, 2007), as well as the *South Dakota Review* and *Graffiti Rag*.

Nelson has taught composition and literature at Auburn University, Augustana College, Albion College, and Henry Ford Community College. She was most recently the Assistant Director of the Hassayampa Institute for Creative Writing at Yavapai College in Prescott, Arizona.

AYAZ DARYL NIELSEN'S poetry has appeared in several literary reviews, including *Lilliput Review, Owen Wister Review, Haight Ashbury Literary Review*, and *Curbside Review*. He is the editor of *bear creek haiku*, which will soon publish its seventy-sixth issue. He is a military veteran, in nursing school, and working toward an M.A. in medical sociology.

JOE PADDOCK is a poet, oral historian, and environmental writer. He thinks of the writing of poetry as work that is ever so important in keeping the soul alive and well. His most recent book of poetry is *A Sort of Honey* (Red Dragonfly Press, 2007).

SUSANNE PETERMANN is a translator and writer living in Southern Oregon. Her most recent book, *Roses & Windows* (self-published in 2006), comprises a selection of Rainer Maria Rilke's French poetry. Between 1982 and 1987, she worked in Casablanca, Morocco as an English teacher. While continuing to translate Rilke's French poems, she works as a freelance professional organizer and mover.

MICHELE HEATHER POLLOCK is a poet and mixed media artist who lives and works in the woods of Indiana. She is the author of two chapbooks of poetry, *Regarding Memory* (Cross Keys Press, 2002) and *A Clean Escape into Something Else* (Sarasota Poetry Theatre Press, 2003). Her work has appeared most recently in *Poetry East*, the *Dos Passos Review*, and *Broken Bridge Review*.

ELISAVIETTA RITCHIE'S books of poetry include *Awaiting Permission to Land* (WordTech Communications, 2006), *The Arc of the Storm* (Signal Books, 1998), *Elegy for the Other Woman* (Signal Books, 1996), *Raking the Snow* (Washington Writers Publishing House, 1982), and *Tightening the Circle Over Eel Country* (Acropolis Books,1974). Her fiction collections include *In Haste I Write You This Note* (Washington Writers Publishing House, 2000) and *Flying Time* (Signal Books, 1992). She edited *The Dolphin's Arc: Endangered Creatures of the Sea* (SCOP Press, Inc., 1986).

BILL ROBERTS is a retired weapons expert who writes poetry to keep his mental machine churning. He lives with one tolerant wife and two spoiled dogs in Broomfield, Colorado. If he had it to do all over again, he'd strive mightily to become either an opera singer or a ballet dancer. Recent publishers of his poetry include the *Atlantic Breast Cancer Net*, *Bellowing Ark*, *Clark Street Review*, *Parnassus Literary Review*, *Red Owl*, *Underground Window*, and *Waterways*, among others.

J. ROMAN is an inmate at the Washington Correctional Facility. He enjoys writing and encouraging teenagers to make the most of their lives.

MICHAEL SHANNON has a B.A. in writing from Kings College and edits technical writing. His creative work has been accepted by *Enigma*, *Steam Ticket*, *Down in the Dirt*, the *Oak*, *AntiMuse*, *Barfing Frog Press*, the *American Drivel Review*, *Transcendental Visions*, *Poetry Motel*, the *Lampshade*, *Cherry Bleeds*, *Zygote in My Coffee*, *Dispatch*, *Straylight*, the *Cherry Blossom Review*, *Backwards City Review*, and the *Foliate Oak*.

DENISE THOMPSON-SLAUGHTER is a writer and freelance editor living in South Bend, Indiana. She has had poetry and nonfiction published in various anthologies and journals, including *California Quarterly*, the *Rambler*, and *Karamu*, and is the winner of the J. Franklin Dew Award (Poetry Society of Virginia) for 2000.

RICK SMITH grew up in New York City but has been in the Los Angeles area for decades, playing and recording on his harmonica, now with the Mescal Sheiks (www.mescalsheiks.com). His poetry has appeared in *Rattle*, *New Letters*, *Onthebus*, *Rhino*, and others. His latest book is *The Wren Notebook* (Lummox Press, 2000). He is also a clinical psychologist specializing in brain damage.

ROGER SMITH'S writings are forthcoming or have been published in *Poetry Motel*, *Skidrow Penthouse*, *Red Hawk Review*, *Red Mountain Review*, *Rhino*, and others.

B.E. STOCK holds a B.A. in creative writing from Sarah Lawrence College. She has studied under E.L. Doctorow, Jane Cooper, Muriel Rukeyser, Maxine Kumin, and Miller Williams. She was a contributor at Bread Loaf Writers Conference in 1970 and 1971. Her work has been widely published in magazines such as *Salt*, *New Press*, *Karamu*, *Wings*, *Array*, *Footwork*, *Spring*, *Piedmont Review*, and others. She has performed frequently in New York cafes and clubs, and has been a featured reader at, among others, the New York Poetry Forum, the Belanthi Gallery, the Shelley Society, Borders, Shakespeare's Sister, the Old Stone House, and the Fall Café. She was a leading reader at the e.e. cummings centennial reading at the Jefferson Market Library in New York City in 1992.

WALLY SWIST'S poems appear or are forthcoming in *Arabesques Review* (Algeria), *New England Watershed* magazine, *Osiris, Rosebud, Sahara: A Journal of New England Poetry*, and the *2008 Lunar Calendar* (Luna Press, 2008). His books of poems include *The New Life* (Plinth Books, 1998), *Veils of the Divine* (Hanover Press, 2003), and *The Silence Between Us* (Brooks Books, 2005). A recording of a poem from his reading in the Sunken Garden Poetry Festival in 2003 is archived at www.npr. org. From September 2003 through August 2005, he was a poet-in-residence at Fort Juniper, the Robert Francis Homestead, in Amherst, Massachusetts.

GABRIELLA TAL has been a lover of Meher Baba (knowingly) for twenty years. She lives in Chapel Hill, North Carolina and makes numerous trips to her Beloved's home in Ahmednagar, India. A therapist and musician, she has written music to many of Bhau Kalchuri's *ghazals*. Her greatest joy is to sing for him. Her CD *Happiness is Better* (2004), produced at Bhau's direction, contains twenty of his *ghazals* sung by herself and other Baba lovers.

BOB TREMMEL teaches at Iowa State University, where he coordinates the teacher education program in the English Department. His work has recently been published by or is forthcoming in *Roanoke Review, Iowa Review, Main Street Rag, Permafrost, River Oak Review, South Dakota Review*, and the *Southwestern Review*. His latest collection is *Crossing Crocker Township* (Timberline Press, 2005).

JON WESICK holds a Ph.D. in physics and has studied Buddhism for twenty years. As such, he has enjoyed a front row seat at a collision of world views. His short stories and novelettes have appeared in *Zahir*, the *American Drivel Review*, the *Aphelion*, *Lullaby*, *Hearse*, *MiniMAG*, *SamizDADA*, *Tidepools*, and *Words of Wisdom*. In addition, Jon has published over a hundred poems in small press journals such as *Pearl*, *Pudding*, and *Slipstream*. His poem "Bread and Circuses" won second place in the African American Writers and Artists contest. Two of his poetry chapbooks have received honorable mentions in the San Diego Book Awards.

KATHERINE WEST makes her home in the mountains near Loveland, Colorado, after having lived most of her adult life in Latin America. She has published one bilingual book, *Native Speakers* (Taller Lenateros, 1998), and has also published a full-length collection of poems based on dreams, *Scimitar Dreams* (Green Fuse Community Press, 2006), with original artwork by Tom Katsimpalis, Curator of Interpretation at the Loveland Museum. Her latest collection is *The Bone Train* (Howling Dog Press, 2007). Her work appears on a regular basis in *New Verse News*, an online poetry newspaper, and has also been published in the *Dickinson Review*, *Poet's* magazine, *Art Word Quarterly*, *White Pelican Review*, and other literary journals. She teaches poetry workshops at the Loveland Museum, Aims Community College, and the Colorado Contemporary Music College in Fort Collins. She also works as poetry editor for *CRONE* magazine and as a member of the editorial collective of Green Fuse Community Press.

BEN WILENSKY'S work has appeared in more than a hundred magazines around the world. Recent publications include *Edge*, *Eureka*, the *Brooklyn Review*, *Envoi UK*, and *Orbis UK*. He is interested in themes of biblical anthropology.

Mr. Wilensky has been a seaman, soldier, and art teacher. He enjoys old and new wines. He has been married for thirty-two years to the love of his life.

FREDRICK ZYDEK is the author of eight collections of poetry. His latest is *T'Kopechuck: The Buckley Poems* (Winthrop Press, 2008). Formerly a professor of creative writing and theology at the University of Nebraska, and later at the College of Saint Mary, he is now a gentleman farmer, when he isn't writing. He is the editor for Lone Willow Press.

asato ma sat gamaya

tamaso ma jyotir gamaya

mrtyor ma amritam gamaya

lead me from illusion to the truth

lead me from darkness to the light

lead me from the noose of death

to the bliss of liberation

lokah samastah sukhino bhavantu

may all beings be happy and free from suffering

om sri gurubhyo namah

i bow to the light within all beings